Crystal & Gemstone Healing
Home Study Course

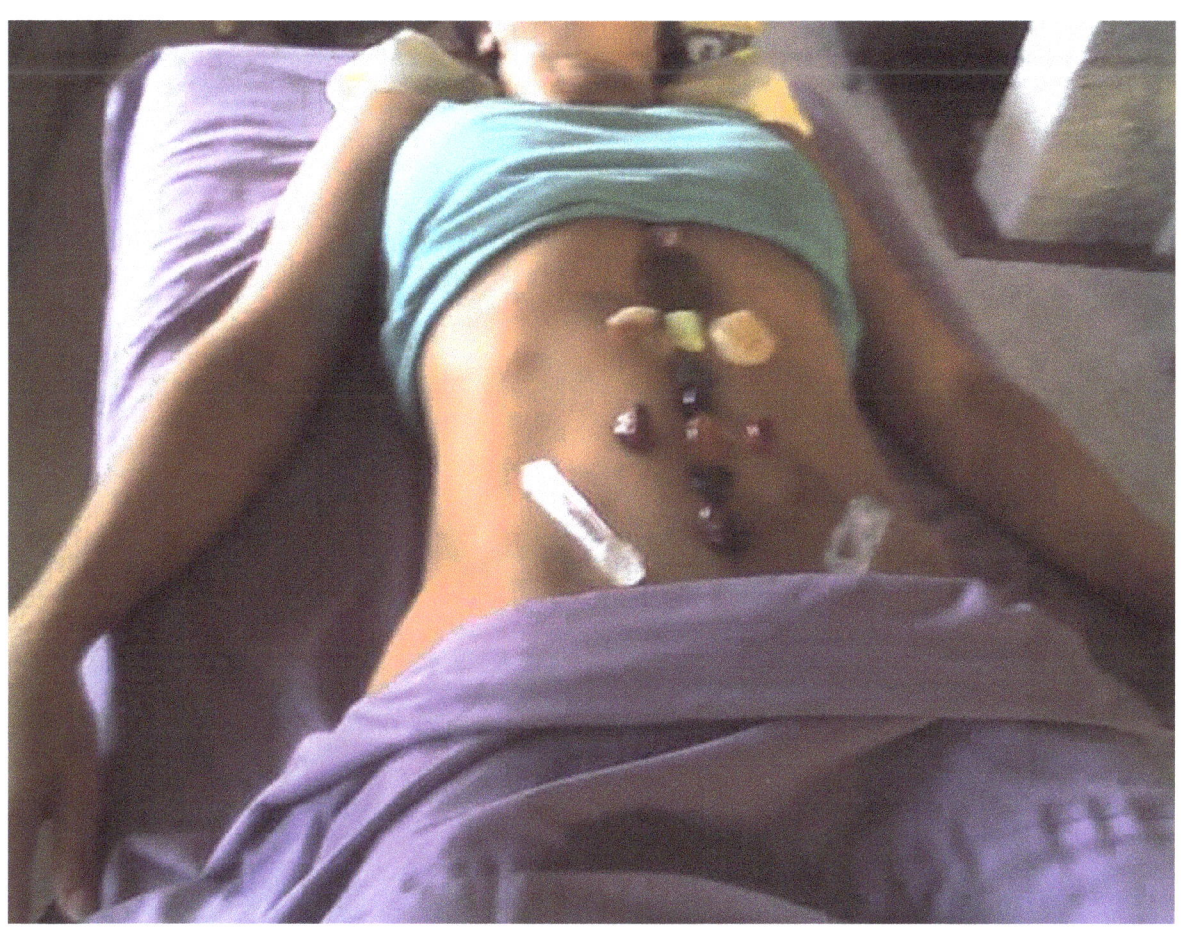

By Charles Lightwalker

Crystal & Gemstone Healing Home Study Course

Author: Charles Lightwalker

Copyright © 2024 Charles Lightwalker

The right of Charles Lightwalker to be identified as author of this work has been asserted by the author in accordance with section 77 and 78 of the Copyright, Designs and Patents Act 1988.

First Published in 2024

ISBN 978-1-83538-279-0 (Paperback)

Published by:
    Maple Publishers
    Fairbourne Drive, Atterbury,
    Milton Keynes,
    MK10 9RG, UK
    www.maplepublishers.com

A CIP catalogue record for this title is available from the British Library.

All rights reserved. No part of this book may be reproduced or translated in any form or by any means, electronic or mechanical, including photocopying, recording or by any information storage and retrieval system without written permission from the author.

This book is a memoir. It reflects the author's recollections of experiences over time. Some names and characteristics have been changed, some events have been compressed, and some dialogues have been recreated, and the Publisher hereby disclaims any responsibility for them.

Copyright © 2012-2024 Charles Lightwalker
All Rights Reserved

No portion of this material may be copied or distributed in any form without the express written permission of the author.

Table of Contents

Beginning Materials:
FORWARD
INTRODUCTION
CERTIFICATION INSTRUCTIONS
STUDY GUIDE

Level One:
WHAT ARE CRYSTALS AND GEMSTONES & HOW ARE THEY FORMED?
HOW DO CRYSTALS WORK?
METAPHYSICAL PROPERTIES
A BRIEF HISTORY OF GEMSTONE HEALING
GEMSTONES & CRYSTALS: CHOOSING, CLEARING, PROGRAMMING, & LAYING
HEALING CHAKRAS
PROTECTION STONES
OTHER ROCK TYPES: IGNEOUS, SEDIMENTARY, & METAMORPHIC

Level Two:
COLOR PSYCHOLOGY & BALANCING THE CHAKRAS WITH COLOR
SACRED HEALING SPACE

Level Three:
A BRIEF HISTORY OF TUNING FORKS
SELECTING AND USING A TUNING FORK
BALANCING THE CHAKRAS & THE ORGANS
USING TUNING FORKS ALONGSIDE CRYSTALS & GEMSTONES

Level Four:
A BRIEF HISTORY OF INTUITIVE EMOTIONAL RELEASE
HOW WE RELEASE EMOTIONS

Level Five:
A BRIEF HISTORY OF REIKI
CRYSTALLINE REIKI
GLOSSARY OF REIKI TERMS

End Materials:
WORKSHEET
DISCLAIMER
LEGAL INFORMATION
ULTIMATE PROTOCOL GUIDE LEVELS 1-5
AFTERTHOUGHTS
ADDENDUM & RECOMMENDED READING
ABOUT THE AUTHOR

Beginning Materials

Introduction
By Lyncara Stewart

'The stone symbolised something permanent that can never be lost or dissolved - Something eternal that men have compared to the mystical experience of God within one's soul' - Carl Jung

Welcome to the works of Charles Lightwalker's crystal and gemstone healing. This comprehensive and revised issue is bound to answer all the thoughts and questions one may have on the topic, plus much more information in addition! Charles has done a great service of including a vast range of knowledge within this book, covering a multitude of workings with crystals.

Charles never fails to amaze. His life story is fascinating alone - Never mind his workings as a medical intuitive, Metis shaman and practitioner, tuning fork therapist, author, and many other talents. Upon meeting Charles and over discussions of our work, he could sense my passion for working with crystals and listened to my plans for sharing 30+ years of experience of my own workings on the subject into publications. He promptly handed me a copy of the Crystal and Gemstone Healing to read. Ever excited to read about my friend's findings on the subject, I was through that book without putting it down!
When I was asked to write a forward for the new and extended publication, I felt it was a great honour to be able to provide Charles with a piece of writing for his great workings within this book. Not just because it is an honour within itself but because of how much I look up to Charles in his field and, more importantly, as a person. His soul and light shine so brightly and this is conveyed in his personality, his truth, his work, and his teachings.

Charles has delivered a comprehensive guide to working with crystals, gemstones, and the mineral kingdom. For the very beginner to the advanced practitioner, there is much information provided for all - Rock types and formations and how they mirror things within ourselves to using more in depth and specified practices such as crystals with Tuning Forks.

No matter where you, the reader, is upon the self healing or crystalline journey this book covers all the bases and provides much insight into working with crystals with not only educational information, but also delving into the esoteric, furthering the field of such workings.

Charles, affectionately known as 'The Networker', is about to network you to the world of the crystal and mineral devas.

Lyncara Stewart
(Mintaka Mermaid)
Holistic Crystal practitioner and author of 'Messages from the Crystal Skulls' and 'Crystals for dreaming and their effects on the subconcious'

Introduction

Welcome to crystal and gemstone healing. I started teaching and writing about crystals, gemstones, and other holistic healing modalities in the late 1990s, but it was not until I started combining various healing methods together into a progressive healing session that I saw the true power that they hold. I called it a progressive healing session because I would start with one modality and then progress to the next that I would intuit was best to provide healing benefits to the client I was working on at the time.

As I employed these progressive healing sessions on clients I noticed deeper emotional, mental, and sometimes even physical changes that dramatically improved people's wellness and overall health. I came to the conclusion that I wanted to write a book about all that I have learned about healing using crystals and gemstones for anyone who wants to learn, but knew that it would not be complete without information about other healing techniques. Throughout this book you will learn about not only crystals and gemstones, but also the ways in which they can be used in tandem with tuning forks, intuitive emotional release, and reiki. This book is a beginning point, offering brief explanations of things which entire books have been written about. I will include further reading recommendations at the end, but for now I hope this book can serve as a jumping off point into holistic healing methods, focusing on gemstones and crystals as promised by the title.

I am continuing to use these different healing techniques in sessions today and I feel truly grateful to the many people who have crossed my path on my journey to writing this book. I hope that you find this book to be both helpful and informative.

Certification Instructions

In order to be certified in Crystal and Stone Healing one needs to complete the following courses:

Level 1- Crystal and Stone Healing
    This basic level introduces one to stones and crystals, and how one
    Can use them in the healing process.

Level 2- Crystal and Stone Healing
    This second level takes one deeper into the realm of healing with crystals and stones.

Level 3- Crystal and Stone Healing with Tuning Forks
    This level show one how to use crystal and stones with tuning
    Forks in a healing process to create deep healing and release.

Level 4- Crystal and Stone Healing with the Intuitive Emotional Release Process.
    This level guides one through the use of Crystals and Stones while using a process designed to release traumas and unwanted

Level 5- Crystal and Stone Healing with Reiki
    This level guides one through combining Reiki with Crystals and Crystals, to create a dynamic healing process.

Study Guide

Home study offers the best way to learn new material because you are able to do the work in your home at your own pace.

You can work at a level you are comfortable with, without rushing to meet deadlines. I advise you to study this material thoroughly, and read all the material repeatedly so that you can develop the knowledge necessary to become the best Crystal and Gemstone Practitioner you can.

I also suggest the following study habits:

> Always study at the same time of day if possible
> Always study for the same amount of time each day
> Meditate daily
> Make your study area a sacred place (set up a sacred healing space)
> Make sure you will not be disturbed during your study time
> Keep a journal of your progress

Level One

What are Crystals and Gemstones & How are they Formed?

Throughout this course/manual, when we refer to crystals we are not speaking of the human-made lead crystals. We are referring to natural crystalline forms, which are grown within Mother Earth.

There are three Kingdoms associated with our earthly plane: the mineral kingdom, the plant kingdom, and the animal kingdom. As we travel upon our life's journey, it is wise for us to rediscover the living power, which exists in the mineral kingdom.

Minerals create materials and machinery used in our modern world, such as transportation, health, etc. It is known in the scientific community that quartz crystals are amplifiers of energy.

As you begin this course open your mind to the ancient secrets that crystals and gemstones hold for us.

What are they Scientifically?

Minerals, crystals and gemstones are composed of the minute particles know as atoms and even further of the particles know as quarks, as is all matter.

As we know, when the basic units of energy examined closely, they are not matter at all, but subtle vibrations, each unit is a being to the cosmic and Universal Life force which is abundant in everything.
The manner in which these individuals particles join together with other particles determines what molecules will form and therefore what matter will exist.

In very crystalline form, such as a clear quartz, or rose quartz, etc. the particles join together in perfect unity and harmony. This integrity also manifests on a molecular level as the pulsating molecules vibrate at the same frequency. This micro-structure, know as the lattice, determines the physical properties of the crystal: its outer shape, hardness, specific gravity, optical properties as well as many other measurable Properties which have long been assigned by those who study geology (some of these are useful to identifying stones and will be discussed at length in Level 2.

The orderly way in which the atoms arrange themselves in any crystalline structure is what makes the resulting object (crystal) complete in and of itself. Each individual unit of energy aligns itself with Universal Life Force and them join with others in a harmony which creates a very purified from of physical matter.

This physical matter vibrates with Universal Life Force energy and the energy of Mother Earth, which formed it.

The mineral kingdom is body of the earth and all that comes from it. We too are Earthly beings and humans are made up of the same elements as the earth, we are NOT separate. Minerals, gemstones and crystals are significant entities, they live, breath, interact, and pulse, emitting vibrations and frequencies which can have a very powerful potential effect on our whole being. They can be sued for transforming, balancing, and attuning body, mind and spirit among many other things.

Most human children are pulled as if by magnetism to stones.
Children will bring stones home to keep, to look at, to hold, to speak to, to sleep with, etc. Children have many uses for stones. As children grow they tend to let go of the attachment to stones because social consciousness.

How they are Formed

From a scientific viewpoint, the Earth formed from a cloud of gasses into a dense fog of dust and then, through contraction, it became denser and shrank into an intensely hot ball which consisted of hot molten matter, called magmas.

The Earth today has cooled enough that it has a crust; however, that crust is still quite thin. If you liken the Earth to an apple, the outer crust of the Earth is about as thick as the skin of an apple. The remainder of the earth is still magma, a glowing hot liquid which is in constant motion.

Not to worry, because there are several miles of rock between your feet and the magma; however this ever changing bio-system contributes enormously to the world of the therapeutic crystals and gemstones.

A Note on Mining

There are two primary ways in which stones are mined.

The first is from rich veins in the earth. Many are mined by amateurs with the simple tools of a hammer and chisel; however, many more are found in large scale operations with expensive explosives and equipment, often in conjunction with mining which is intended to recover coal, or other minerals. Quartz crystals are most often mined in this way.

The second method is retrieval of crystals which are concentrated in deposits on the surface of the earth, often in areas of water such as streams of river beds. These deposits are known as placer deposits which are composed of fragments of decomposed veins. This method is most often done on a small scale by placing stones in a sieve and shaking or using water to separate the heavier gravel from the crystals; however, it can be done in a large scale mining operation as well.

How do Crystals Work?

No one seems to know for sure. Stories tell that they were first used in Atlantis (I used them during one of my incarnation there). Crystals became important to the people of that civilization who believed in their capacity to store and amplify any power source fed into them - physical, mental, emotional, or spiritual. Practitioners of modern-day crystal therapy believe that the stones' ability to work as conductors allow them to focus energy via a person's thoughts to stimulate healing - both physical and non-physical.

However, in addition to medical controversy as to their efficacy, the use of crystals for healing is not an exact science. There is plenty of information available to describe which crystals and gemstones are good for treating certain ailments or for the prevention of certain conditions. The problem is that much of it appears contradictory. Still, thousands of people throughout the world swear by the use of crystals for a variety of mental, emotional, and physical problems. There are numerous claims that they aid such in diverse areas as harmonious relationships, allergies, and spiritual awakening.

Crystals are used in meditation and spiritual ceremonies, laid on the body during types of massage or bodywork, when a person is resting, or placed in drinking or bathing waters. It is claimed that an odd number of facets on the stone aid in healing, while an even number of facets create the best energizers. Red, yellow, and orange stones are said to produce energy, clear and aquamarine stones are healers, and lavender and blue-violet stones create calming effects.

Metaphysical Properties

Here is a list of gemstones, and there metaphysical properties. I use many of these gemstones is my healing work:

Agate: Balances ying-yang energy, stabilizes the aura. Facilitates discernment. Imparts strength and courage. Opens one to innate creative talents. (There are many forms of agate, each with specific properties.)

Amber: Purifies body, mind, and spirit. Balances electromagnetics of the body and allows even flow of energies. Provides a positive, soothing energy. Spiritualizes the intellect.

Amethyst: Sedative energy. Facilitates spirituality and contentment. Stone of stability, strength, and peace. Excellent for meditation. Enhances psychic ability.

Aventurine: Independence, leadership, creativity. Balances male/female energies. Aligns mental, physical, emotional, and auric bodies.

Aurauralite: Protection absorbs all negativity and transmutes it, and it never needs to be cleansed.

Aquamarine: Courage, intellect, protection. Assists spiritual awareness, actualization.

Azurite: Awakens psychic ability, insight, intuition. Third eye. Excellent for clearing the mind in meditation.

Apache Tears: Assists in the grieving process, and allows forgiveness. Breaks down the barriers that hold one back. Also good for the analytical mind.

Amazonite: Balancing energy, harmony, universal love.

Calcite: Energy amplifier, teacher. Optical Calcite is excellent for clearing and cleansing.
Celestite Excellent stone for dream recall and astral travel. Hope and harmony. Communication.
Chrysocolla: Strength, balance. Promotes harmony and attunement to the earth. Purifies one's environment.

Chrysoprase: Balances yin-yang energy. Acceptance of self and others. Citrine: Positive energy - stone needs no cleansing . Dissipates negative energy. Warmth, joy, optimism.

Copal: Excellent for strengthening the abilities of the mind, and altered states of consciousness. Amplifies one's energy field.

Diamond: Purity, perfection, abundance, inspiration.

Emerald: Loyalty, sensitivity, harmony, tranquility. Assists in memory retention and mental clarity.

Fluorite: Stability, order, discernment, concentration. Helps one to understand and maintain ideals and the perfection of the universe.

Garnet: Commitment, devotion, love, stability and order. Even flow of energy.

Gold: Spirituality, understanding, attunement to nature. Attracts positive energy. Excellent healer.

Hematite: Excellent for the mind. Grounding.

Herkimer Diamond: Awareness, attunement, clairvoyance, telepathy. Good for information retention.

Jade: Harmony, peace, fidelity, confidence. A wonderful dream stone. Jasper: Protection, awareness, insight. Grounding.

Kunzite: Communication, love, peace. Protects and dissolves negativity. Excellent for meditation.

Kyanite: Never needs cleaning or clearing, aligns all chakras. Tranquility, communication, psychic awareness. Excellent for meditation and dream recall.

Labradorite: Represents the light of the universe, extra-terrestrial energy. Intuition, subconscious. Illumination.

Lapis Lazuli: Knowledge, wisdom, perfection, protection, creative expression.

Lepidolite: Honesty, stability, hope, acceptance. Assists in change and transition. Facilitates astral travel.

Malachite: Transformation, spiritual development. Clears the way to attain goals. Fidelity, loyalty, reasoning ability.

Moldavite: Clarity, eternity. Extra-terrestrial, inter-dimensional access. Moonstone: Lunar, female energy. Emotional, intuitive. Rhythms, cycles, destiny.

Obsidian: Dispels negativity. Grounding, healing, protective. Helps one to clearly see one's flaws and the changes that are necessary.

Onyx: Centering, self-control, intuitive guidance. Assists in the grieving process.

Opal: Creativity, inspiration, imagination.

Peridot: Healing, protective. Allows one to understand changes in one's life, regulates life cycles.

Petrified Wood: Grounding, provides strength. Stone of transformation. Pyrite: Shields from negative energy, good stone of protection. Enhances intellect and memory. Symbol of the sun.

Quartz Crystal (clear): Universal crystal, clarity of consciousness. Rhodochrosite: Love energy. Excellent stone for balance in all areas.

Ruby: Loving, nurturing, spirituality, wealth, protection

Rutilated Quartz: Intensifies energy of the crystal. Stimulates brain. Inspiration, clairvoyance.

Sapphire: Joy, peace, beauty, prosperity.

Selenite: (Gypsum) Clarity of consciousness, awareness, insight, good judgment. Aids in accessing past/future lives.

Silver: Mirror to the soul. Eloquence. Connects physical and astral bodies. In jewelry, it provides a balanced setting that retains the qualities of the stone it holds. Lunar energy. Cleansing, balancing.

Smoky Quartz: Dissolves negativity, grounding, balancing. Excellent for meditation.

Sodalite: Logic, efficiency, truthfulness. Enhances group communication. Sugilite: Spiritual love, perfection, inspiration, confidence. Alleviates negative/destructive emotions.

Tiger's eye: Earthy, grounding. Represents sun and earth. Optimism, insight, personal power.

Topaz: Success, true love, individuality, creativity, joy.

Tourmaline: Inspiration, understanding, self-confidence, balancing. Electrical.

Tourmalinated Quartz: Strength, balancing. Combines attributes of tourmaline and quartz

Turquoise: Spiritual attunement, strength, grounding. Protective - excellent for astral travel.

Zircon: Virtue, unification, continuity, purity.

A Brief History of Gemstone Healing

Throughout history and legend, people from all cultures and continents have used the spiritual and healing powers of gems, stones and crystals. From as far back as the days of the legendary lost city of Atlantis, through the ancient Mayan and Hebrew civilizations, and including Far Eastern, Native American and Celtic cultures, crystals and gemstones have been used for religious purposes as well as communion, physical and spiritual healing, the power of gems and crystals is intertwined with the history of mankind. It is widely believed that gems, stones, & crystals act as amplifiers when brought into contact with the human body's seven-chakra points. Rotating at different speeds, these chakra points release energies, imparting the body with its precious life forces.

While your chakras can become clogged from stress or anxiety, using gems or crystals in accordance with meditation or bodywork is thought to help balance these energy points, promoting health, happiness and well being. While it is not recommended that gems, stones or crystals be used in place of modern medical treatment, many people find that the use of healing gems improves their overall well being, encouraging a more positive outlook and a generally healthier visage.

Gems, stones, or crystals can be used interchangeably for healing purposes. They are commonly chosen to aid specific ailments but many people find that they don't choose their gem, stone, or crystal, it chooses them. While casually perusing gems and crystals you may find that a particular item draws you to it. Follow your instincts. Your body needs all 7 color rays: red, orange, yellow, green, blue, indigo and violet; and you may unconsciously be drawn to the gems, stones, or crystals that are most appropriate for you. Alternatively, you may choose a gem, stone or crystal that relates to one of your energy centers or chakras that is in need of clearing, balancing or enhancing.

The primary use for gems throughout history has been for healing and spiritual rituals. Although gems were rare and exhibited great beauty, the reason they were so precious was due to the power they imparted to their wearers. They are storehouses of empowerment, transmitted through contact with one's body. Kings and queens would have gemstones set in their crowns to obtain their potencies. They connected the monarchs with forces enabling them to rule guided by cosmic energies. Priests of different religions used gems in rings for similar reasons. Shamans used gemstones in healing and other rituals.

Gems exhibit their power in a beneficial or detrimental way - depending on how they are used. The inherent powers of gemstones are recognized by modern science in the technological uses of crystals in watches, lasers, and computers, but the more subtle potencies, such as their ability to promote physical healing in the body, or their power to help balance human emotions, elude modern science. Here are few points I wish to make regarding gemstones.

1) All stones or gems have magnetic powers in varying degrees, and many of them are beneficial to us for their therapeutic cures.

2) They emit vibrations and frequencies, which have strong potential influence on our whole being.

3) They create strong energy fields, which enable us to be charged with their energies.

4) The gems are used for healing, transforming, balancing, and attuning the body, mind and soul.

5) They are a manifestation of vibrancy, light and color, life, textures, transparency and clarity.

6) They activate our abilities, soothe and comfort, heal and balance through the purity of their rays.

7) The patterns in the stones reveal to us the changes that keep taking place, indicating that life is change - that the process of evolution is a cosmic law.

8) Each gem, tuned to a particular ray, has a special role to play.

9) Gems can be cleaned by leaving them under running water for six hours. Or, bury them in some earth overnight, and rinse them off. Or, keep the stone in the flame of a candle until the

candle melts. Or still, place the stone amongst a heap of quartz for several days, whereby its energy is revived from the contact of the quartz.

10) The gem that is cleaned should be placed in direct sunlight, for the sun is a great source of energy and purification.

11) The more precious stones that you wear, the more strongly will you be charged with cosmic forces, radiating out into your surroundings.

12) Wear your stones - Do not store them in a safe or jewelry box, for you will be depriving your body of their tremendous power.

13) Precious stones have a way of healing emotions that have been inharmonious.

14) The stones selected for use should always be in contact with one's body to absorb their healing properties.

15) Stones should be carried in a Medicine bag to provide healing to others when needed. All shamans and Medicine people carried stones as a way to provide healing to others in times of illness, during ancient times.

16) Create a talisman to wear with your gemstones. A Talisman is any object, design or symbol known to be in possession of magical or divine power of its own which is transmitted to the wearer.

Gemstones & Crystals: Choosing, Clearing, Programming, & Laying

Choosing

Remember that Crystals, Minerals and Gemstones are living, breathing beings and just as with other relationship which enrich you, there is a need for connection with your stones.

It is important to open your heart to the stones. Trust your intuition and your feeling. Do Not Use Your Mind to Explain or rationalize.

Have you ever listened very closely to hear a special secret from a very important friend? This is how you should open your heart and mind to communicate with crystals gemstones.

Drop any preconceived notions, expectations or fears that it cannot be done and allow the inner mind to receive the subtle impressions that the stone emanates.

Open yourself to the possibility that these life forms want to share their secrets and wisdom with you. With no doubt in your mind, accept the images, which come into your consciousness.

You may wish to have a stone that is tuned to your zodiac sign, but don't limit yourself to only that stone.

Let your Higher Self guide you to the stone that you need at any point in time because of its particular color or properties. As you ponder your choices, one or two stones will usually call your attention strongly. These are stones that to go with you.

Simply put. Take the one to which you are most drawn to. That particular gemstone, crystal or stone will always be what you need at that moment in time. Intention always helps, if you know for what purpose the stone will be used, you will be drawn to the best stone for that purpose.

Stones come in many forms, and as long as the stone is natural rather human made, all the forms are positive for healing. Some people prefer rough specimens just as they come from the Earth, while others prefer specimens, which have been polished or even cut and faceted. Some may prefer using smooth, tumbled stones, eggs, wands, sphere or even those, which are carved.

Stones come in all sizes and grades. Pick the size that is comfortable for you to use and the grade that is attractive both in price and ascetics. Stones with clearer colors have stronger energy, as do stones that are larger in size; but, all natural stones have healing energy.

You may use stones for decoration in your healing environment. They can be placed under a healing table or on an altar and many times larger stones are better for this purpose. Smaller stones are can be carried in pockets or held in hands while meditating or sleeping. When used in healing, they can be laid on the body such as over the chakras or even taped to the skin.

Gemstones can also be made into elixirs and essences or used as pendulums.

Clearing

To clear a gemstone or crystal means cleansing it of extraneous energy from others, that it may be holding.

Stones absorb energy from anyone who handles them, and quartz crystals and many gemstones heal pain by taking it into themselves. If these unwanted energies are left in the stone, it will affect its ability to use as a healing tool. Very overloaded stones sometimes self-destruct, shattered or get lost. Remember, uncleared stones can transmit another person's pain to the next person who holds the stone. The clearer the energy of healing stone, the more useful it is.

Stones used for healing or in Laying on of stones are used intentionally to absorb others' pain. Stones should be cleared after every use in healing.

Clearing Methods

1. *Salt* is the most powerful method for clearing crystals. Salt can be used dry or dissolved in water. To use salt water, mix a tablespoon of organic sea salt, in a glass or ceramic cup or small bowl of cold water. Place the stones to be cleared in the salt-water solution and allow them to soak overnight. To use dry salt, place dry sea salt in a glass bowl or non-plastic container and bury the stones to be cleared in the salt. Leave overnight. You can also wash the stones in the ocean if you live near the sea.

2. Placing them in *sunlight*, or in *moonlight* can also clear stones. Bright sun clears stones beautifully in an hour. Stones can be left outdoors on full moon nights for clearing.

3. Try hanging gemstones from the branches of a tree in the *rain*, dry or night, twelve hours in recommended.

4. Stones can be buried in the *ground* and left there for a period of time, which is especially good for highly over loaded healing tools. You can place them in a flowerpot filled with soil. Leave the stone or stones in the earth for a full moon cycle, from Dark Moon to Dark Moon.

5. Various *herbs* can also be used to clear crystals and gemstones. The herbs can either be used dry or burned for their smoke. Stones may be buried in dry herbs such as rose petals, sage, cedar, or frankincense. Smudging a stone is when the stone is passed thru the smoke of herbs that is burning. For stones to heal a human energy field, they must be able to transmit their highest and most positive vibration possible. Only cleared stones offer this high vibrational frequency of healing.

Programming

After you clear your gemstones or crystals, you should program them. This is a very simple process. Hold the stone in your hand, or touch it if it is too large to hold, and sense its energy. As you sense the stone pr crystal's energy and appreciate it, ask quietly to be connected to the diva of that particular piece. Remember stones are living things, and the diva of the piece is the stone's life force energy.

Once you feel you have sensed what you can from the energy, think of what you will use the stone for. Will you use it for healing, or protection? For healing yourself or others? Think of these uses, and then ask the gemstone if it is willing to act in the way you wish.

You should have some idea if there is a yes or no response. The crystal's energy may increase with a yes or seem to disappear with a no. I use most of my stones for healing. If the stone accepts your intent, state in your mind that it be so.

What you have just done with the gemstone is to "program" it, like programming a computer.

Thank the stone for accepting this programming. If you are a Crystaline Reiki Master symbols work beautifully to clear or program the stone. Also place the stone or crystal inside the sacred healing space* while programming the piece. Hold the stone in your hand, sense its energy, and then focus the symbols into them.

The purpose of programming a crystal or gemstone is to focus its abilities on something you specifically need, thereby magnifying the stone's intent through your own. A crystal or stone that is programmed in these ways become much more powerful and useful as a healing tool.

Laying

The technique of using crystals and gemstones on the client's body for healing is called lying on of stones.

It is a powerful method of clearing negative energy, clearing and balancing the chakras, releasing emotional toxicity.

The crystals or gemstones move the client's vibrations into alignment with the universal grid. This results in a freeing of life force energy in the chakras, auric body, and transformation of disease into health.

The stones can be used in hands on healing session or alone. I prefer using the stones in conjunction with hands on healing, as I believe the session is more powerful.

To begin the client lies on the healing table, face up with a pillow under the head and knees for comfort. The stones are then placed on the client's body.

Healing Chakras

Crystal or gem varieties are believed to have positive effects when utilized on particular energy centers or chakras of the body, much like deep therapeutic massage and acupuncture. The 7 basic chakra points of the human body, their locations and general attributes are as follows:

1. **Root Chakra**

Location: The base of the spine
Color: Red

- Physical Association: Adrenal glands, kidneys, spinal column, back, hips, legs and feet.
- Spiritual Aspects: Stability, security, grounding, courage and physical and emotional survival.
- When The Chakra Point Is Blocked: Anxious, fearful, angry and frustrated.
- Gems & Crystals That Work With This Chakra: Cornelian, Garnet, Ruby, Cuprite, Black Tourmaline, Smoky Quartz, Onyx, Agate, Black Obsidian, Hematite, Fire Agate, Ametrine, Blood Stone and Nephrite.

2. **Sacral Chakra**

Location: Lower abdomen to navel
Color: Orange

- Physical Association: Genital area, reproductive organs, bladder, bowel and lower intestine.
- Spiritual Aspects: Creativity, harmony, emotional balance, passion, sexuality, freedom and expression of emotions.
- When The Chakra Point Is Blocked: Stiff lower back, restlessness, confusion and sexual blockages.
- Gems & Crystals That Work With This Chakra: Amber, Moonstone, Cornelian, Citrine, Golden Topaz, Golden Beryl, Aragonite, Orange Calcite, Selenite, Zircon and Sunstone.

3. **Solar Plexus Chakra**

Location: Below the ribs to 3 inches above the navel

Color: Yellow

- Physical Association: Stomach, pancreas and liver.
- Spiritual Aspects: Personal power, strength, sense of self worth, transformation, courage and laughter.
- When The Chakra Point Is Blocked: Expression of anger, fear and hate.
- Gems & Crystals That Work With This Chakra: Citrine, Golden Topaz, Green-Yellow Tourmaline, Tiger's Eye, Heliodor, Rutilated Quartz, Amber, Sunstone, Malachite, Peridot and Emerald.

4. **Heart Chakra**

Location: Center of the chest
Color: Green

- Physical Association: Heart, lungs and thymus gland
- Spiritual Aspects: Unconditional love, forgiveness and compassion.
- When The Chakra Point Is Blocked: Emotional instability.
- Gems & Crystals That Work With This Chakra: Rose Quartz, Pink Tourmaline, Rubellite, Rhodochrosite, Emerald, Green Tourmaline, Malachite, Morganite, Kunzite, Green Aventurine, Ruby, Hiddenite, Grossular Garnet, Green Jade, Nephrite, Kunzite, Prehnite, Chrysoprase, Rhodonite, Moldavite, Prasiolite, Watermelon Tourmaline and other natural green gems.

5. **Throat Chakra**

Location: Throat area
Color: Blue

- Physical Association: Mouth, throat, thyroid and parathyroid glands
- Spiritual Aspects: communication, truthfulness, expression of will power and creativity.
- When The Chakra Point Is Blocked: Headaches, tension within the neck and shoulder muscles, colds, thyroid or hearing problems.
- Gems & Crystals That Work With This Chakra: Apophyllite, Aquamarine, Blue Lace Agate, Blue Topaz, Blue Tourmaline, Celestite, Indicolite, Blue Turquoise, Chrysocolla, Amazonite, Lapis Lazuli, Larimar, Sodalite, Iolite, Kyanite and Zircon.

6. **Brow (Third Eye) Chakra**

Location: Center of the forehead
Color: Purple

- Physical Association: Pituitary gland, pineal gland, skull, eyes, brain and nervous system.
- Spiritual Aspects: Coordination, balance, mental clarity, clairvoyance, intuition, wisdom.
- When The Chakra Point Is Blocked: Blindness, headaches, nightmares, eyestrain or blurred vision Associated.
- Gems & Crystals That Work With This Chakra: Azurite, Sugilite, Amethyst, Celestite, Tanzanite, Blue Tourmaline, Sapphire, Lavender Quartz, Purple Fluorite, Charoite, Sodalite, and Iolite.

7. Crown Chakra
Location: Top center of the head
Color: Violet

- Physical Association: Pineal gland, top of spinal cord and brain stem.
- Spiritual Aspects: Spirituality and life force energy
- When The Chakra Point Is Blocked: Depression, alienation, confusion, and inability to learn or comprehend.
- Gems & Crystals That Work With This Chakra: Sugilite, Ametrine, Clear Quartz Crystal, Amethyst, Howlite, Moonstone, Lavender Quartz, Rutilated Quartz, Diamond and White Topaz.

8. Omega Chakra
Location: half way between the knees and the pelvis
Color: Infared

- Spiritual Aspects: Divine Feminine energy.
- When The Chakra Point Is Blocked: Anxious, fearful, angry, and hateful.
- Gems & Crystals That Work With This Chakra: Cornelian, Garnet, Ruby, Cuprite, Black Tourmaline, Smoky Quartz, Onyx, Agate, Black Obsidian, Hematite, Fire Agate, Ametrine, Blood Stone, Rutilated Quartz,

Amber, Sunstone, Malachite, Peridot and Emerald.

9. Alpha Chakra
Location: 6 inches above the crown of the head
Color: Ultraviolet

- Spiritual Aspects: Potential, because it is the beginning of all possibilities.
- When The Chakra Point Is Blocked: Headaches, Depression, alienation, confusion, tension within the neck and shoulder muscles, colds, thyroid or hearing problems.
- Gems & Crystals That Work With This Chakra: Sugilite, Ametrine, Clear Quartz Crystal, Amethyst, Howlite, Moonstone, Lavender Quartz, Rutilated Quartz, Apophyllite, Aquamarine, Blue Lace Agate, Blue Topaz, Blue Tourmaline, Celestite, Indicolite, Blue Turquoise, Chrysocolla,

Amazonite, Lapis Lazuli, Diamond and White Topaz.

10. Terra Chakra
Location: Between the ankles and the heel of the foot.
Color: Silver

- Spiritual Aspects: This chakra is 3rd dimensional and it is where creation can occur, where solid and physical mass exist.
- When The Chakra Point Is Blocked: Anxious, fearful, angry, frustrated, Stiff lower back, restlessness, confusion and sexual blockages.
- Gems & Crystals That Work With This Chakra: Cornelian, Garnet, Ruby, Cuprite, Black Tourmaline, Smoky Quartz, Onyx, Agate, Black Obsidian, Hematite, Fire Agate, Blood Stone, Nephrite, Amber,

Moonstone, Cornelian, Citrine, Golden Topaz, Golden Beryl, Aragonite, Selenite, Zircon and Sunstone.

11. **Angelic Chakra**
Location: 12 inches above the top of the head
Color: Gold

- Spiritual Aspects: Absolute knowledge, absolute wisdom and absolute love.
- When The Chakra Point Is Blocked: Blindness, headaches, nightmares, eyestrain, Depression, alienation, confusion, and inability to learn or comprehend.
- Gems & Crystals That Work With This Chakra: Azurite, Sugilite, Amethyst, Celestite, Tanzanite, Blue Tourmaline, Sapphire, Lavender Quartz, Purple Fluorite, Charoite, Sodalite, and Iolite.

Protection Stones

Crystals and stones have given their metaphysical energies to protect people for aeons. From amber which was used extensively for protection by the ancient Romans to golden amulets of the ancient Egyptians to modern good luck charms, many protection magic items have been made of crystals and stones of various kinds.

General Protection Lore: agate, alum, amber (used extensively by Ancient Romans), apache tears, aventurine, banded agate, beryl, black agate, black kyanite, black obsidian, black tourmaline, calcite, carnelian, cat's eye, chalcedony, chrysoprase, citrine, chiastolite, coral, emerald, fire agate, flint, fluorite, fossils, gold, golden topaz, halite (rock salt crystal), heliodor (golden beryl), hematite, herkimer diamond, holey stones, honey calcite, imperial topaz, jade, jasper, jet, labradorite, lapis (lapis lazuli), lava, lepidolite, magnesite (lodestone), mahogany obsidian, malachite, marble, mookaite, moonstone, nuumite, ocean jasper, olivine, pearl, peridot, petrified wood, prehnite, pumice, pyrite, quartz, quartz crystal clusters, red jasper, ruby, rutilated quartz, salt, sapphire, sard, sardonyx, selenite, serpentine, shark teeth, snowflake obsidian, staurolite, sulphur, sunstone, tiger's eye, topaz, tourmaline (red and black especially), tree agate, turitella agate, turquoise, yellow agate, yellow jasper, zircon (clear and red).

Protection from Evil Lore: agate (especially Eye Agate), beryl, black tourmaline, blue chalcedony (especially evil magick), coral, garnet, herkimer diamond, malachite, pyrite, quartz, salt, sapphire, snowflake obsidian, tiger iron / mugglestone (mirrors evil & evil spells back to the sender), turquoise.

Protection from Negativity/Negative Energies Lore: black kyanite, black obsidian, black onyx, black tourmaline (transmutes to positive energy), bornite, celestite, citrine, elestial crystals, jet (absorbs negative energies), katanganite, kunzite, peacock ore, plancheite, quartz, smoky quartz (especially in healing).

Protection for Children Lore: agate (especially blue lace agate and green moss agate), jade, malachite (especially from evil eye and evil spirits), mother of pearl (newborn infants in particular), ruby (all family, including children)

Protection During Childbirth & Pregnancy Lore: ammonite, chrysocolla (especially for preventing miscarriage), geodes, hematite, lepidolite, malachite, moonstone, picture jasper (during childbirth especially), rose quartz

Protection for Homes & Other Buildings Lore: aurauralite, halite, holey stones, salt, riverstone, quartz, ruby, witches fingers.

Physical Protection Lore: aurauralite, carnelian, agate, fluorite, peridot, sard, smoky quartz, zircon

Protection During Physical Travel Lore: amethyst, aquamarine (travel upon water), chalcedony, garnet, herkimer diamond, jet, malachite (esp when flying), moonstone (travel at sea), mother of pearl (on water), pearl (on water) rainbow moonstone, tiger's eye, petalite, yellow jasper.

Psychic Protection Lore: aurauralite, amber (psychic shielding), amethyst (from negative psychic energy of all kinds), black obsidian, DT crystals, elestial crystals (esp psychic attacks), fluorite, jade (especially vs psychic attack), lapis lazuli, Lemurian seed crystal, moqui marbles / moki balls (esp during shamanic work), nuumite, prehnite, pyrite, ruby, seraphinite (serafina, chlinochlore), sugilite, tiger iron / mugglestone (especialy during shamanic work)

Here is a list of a few stones and crystals I have used for protection:

- Clear quartz crystals have many amazing properties. They are transmitters and receivers of energy. Because of this, they can be used as aids in healing work. They also capable of storing and holding energy for a long period of time. This makes them ideal to use as protection.

- Pyrite is a wonderful stone that can be used for protection. When placed near the body it emits a vibrational energy that surrounds the body's energy field with protection form negative energy.

- Aurauralite, a mysterious stone that absorbs negative energy and transmutes it. The stone never has to be cleared, and is quite useful during healing session for the client to hold while you are doing energy healing work, intuitive emotional release work, crystaline reiki, quantum touch, gemstone healing, sound healing, and other healing modalities.

Protection stones help us separate what is ours energetically from what belongs to someone else. Instead of erecting psychic barriers that shut others out, including those we love and want to be our friends, we can use stones as protection, to help us maintain a boundary that allows love, joy, and peace to enter while deflecting energies that do not serve or support us. This has the additional benefit of freeing up energy we have been using to erect and maintain barriers, reducing internal stress and fatigue. We can use stones to protect dwelling spaces, businesses, schools and outdoor areas as well as individuals. To learn more about stones, crystals and other healing or protective gemstones attend one of my workshops on Learning how to use these valuable tools.

Stones are here to help us. As one Hawaiian Shaman said to me "Your stone finds you." Stones help you connect with the earth's "mana"(life force energy).

Today stones are becoming more and more popular, as the increase of crystal and gemstone stores increase so does the interest in "Stone Healing" workshops.

Each stone, just like each person, has it's own vibration. That vibration helps people tune into the old knowledge contained in the stone.

OTHER ROCK TYPES: IGNEOUS, SEDIMENTARY, & METAMORPHIC

IGNEOUS

The formation of minerals from magma is like the emergence of sugar crystals in jelly which is over saturated with sugar. It is a proven scientific principle that hot liquids are able to dissolve larger quantities of solids than cold liquids. The sugar in the hot jelly was dissolved; however, as the jelly cooled, the sugar crystals became apparent.

Crystallization of minerals from magma occurs in exactly the same way. Magma is a mass of molten rock. Once magma begins to cool down, it cannot retain all the different substances in the solution and some of the matter begins to move out of the liquid.
This process begins with small "seeds" that gradually grow into larger material and it continues until, as the end of the cooling phase, all liquid matter has become solid.

If the end product consists of matter which is all the same, we call it a mineral; but, if it consists of a mixture of substances (several minerals), we call it rock. The size of the crystals in the end product will depend upon how quickly the magma cools down, which is the same time the magma has had available for the mineral's growth.
This explains why crystals of minerals which are created during a magma eruption (a volcano) are considered smaller than those which formed deep with in the Earth.
In mineralogy, the rock and minerals that have formed directly from magma are called igneous or magmatic rocks and minerals.

Depending upon where they were formed, whether at the surface or deep in the Earth, igneous rocks are divided into rocks or minerals of volcanic origin (vulcanites and volcanic minerals) and rocks of plutonic origin (plutonites, otherwise known as "intrusive" rocks) Rocks of plutonic origin are further divided into three sub-categories, called liquid-magmatic, pneumatolytic and hydrothermal.

Igneous: Vulcanites

These are usually formed as fine-grained rocks containing minerals that produce minute crystals. The most well known of these are the lightweight, "lava rocks", such as pumice, and basalt. Among the healing crystals formed this way are porphyrites, and rhyolites and fire opal.

In some cases, lava rock cools extremely quickly, such as when it steams into cold water and many times, no crystals are formed at all. Instead the entire mass is practically frozen by the shock of the temperature and it forms a glass-like mass. This is how Obsidian is formed. Strictly speaking, Obsidian is not counted among minerals, because it is a mixture of several substances, it is primarily classified as a rock and is often called rock glass or volcanic glass.

It is the variance of composition which makes obsidian vary from simple black to mahogany, rainbow, silver, and snowflake.

Igneous: Plutonites

Plutonites are minerals which do not form at the same time. The first minerals start forming freely in the liquid magma where they will either sink down or move up depending upon their density. This is how certain minerals accumulate at certain depths and become concentrated.

The initial step in mineral formation is called "liquid magmatic formation" which simply means "the formation of minerals from liquid magma". This process occurs at between 1100 and 700 degrees Celsius and under enormous pressure. Examples of minerals formed this way are aventurine, epidote, oblivine, peridot, rose quartz and hyacinth zircon.

Sometimes, gases or vapors from the magma penetrate neighboring rocks and this way also leads to mineral formation through substances dissolving out of the rock and forming compounds with the gases from the magma. This is known as "pneumatolytic formation". The following are formed as a result of this: apatite, lepidolite, topaz and tourmaline.

During the cooling phase following the above and once critical temperature of water at 375 degrees Celsius and below is reached, aqueous solutions result. At temperatures above this critical temperature, water is present only as vapor no matter the pressure; however, below this temperature, water can become liquid if the pressure is great enough and then further minerals are formed from the substances dissolved in the water. This is known as "hydrothermal formation". Among crystals formed from this pressure are: amazonite, aragonite, fluorite, and moonstone.

Water is much more free-flowing than magma and it is able to more easily penetrate into cracks in surrounding rock material. The minerals here occur as "drus" on the walls of cavities in the surrounding rock and form "guangue rocks". This mineral solutions in this formation cool very slowly due to the insulating properties of the surrounding rock and they also have plenty of space to grow undisturbed which means that they are able to from large crystals. Some examples of this formation are agate, amethyst, rock crystal, chalcedony and smoky quartz.

Igneous: Healing Properties

If we consider the formation of this class of rocks and minerals, we will realize that our human lives contain many similar processes. From the first moments of our birth, we are occupied with learning . It is amazing when one views the learning accomplishments of young children among which are grasping, sitting, standing, walking, talking, and recognizing other people. These are all complex matters and are learned in such a short period of time that we must realize that the tendencies for all of the above were there from the start.

These natural abilities are among those things that distinguish us from other species. We can talk, but not fly like a bird. These natural abilities are part of our natural tendencies, whether they are apart of spiritual inheritance or genetic.

This is very similar to the formation of Igneous rock, in that the magma contains the basic elements which are then formed through the specific processes. However; the formation would not occur unless the tendencies were contained within the magma in the beginning.

Additionally, what good are these natural tendencies if we do no have the time, space and energy to develop them further? Just as with igneous rocks, time, space and energy are an important part of their formation and development.

Minerals and rocks do not change our birth tendencies; however, they can help us to develop our inner potential. Igneous rocks, particularly primary minerals, will encourage learning processes, due to the similar manner of their origin.

Every igneous rock and primary mineral represents a certain spiritual value and will support and encourage certain kinds of spiritual experiences and the corresponding thought and behavior patterns and if it is for the highest good will bring about healing of these values, thoughts, experiences and behavior patterns.

Primary minerals are the first choice of healing stones, when we are faced with learning experiences or when we are being confronted with new ideas or we have chosen a path of new beginning.

Sedimentary

Rocks which form are on the surface of the Earth where it becomes abundantly clear that stones and rocks do not remain the same forever are sedimentary rocks. As time passes, sun, rain and snow, heat, and cold, frost and wind gnaw away at the rock. This action is called "erosion or weathering".

As mountains are worn down by weather, rocks split off and turn into huge gravel slopes found on mountains. This gravel will gradually move toward the bottom of the slope where flowing water then transform the angular pieces of rock into round pebbles by rolling them against each other.

During this process, many small fragments create sand. Some small amounts of mineral forming elements may be dissolved in the water, into chalk or rock salt. This is large scale weathering.

Water transports matter as long as it flows. When it slows down it will deposit anything it has carried along. Vast deposits, out of which new rock is formed, build up this way. These are called sedimentary rocks and among then are angelisite, achydrite, calcite, dolomite, oolite, Selenite and pyrite. This is sedimentation.

Any rocks close to the surface of the earth are penetrated by water which carries oxygen, carbon dioxide and acids with it. As this water penetrates, it begins to dissolve the rock and release mineral-forming elements. This occurs whether the rock is exposed to air or covered

with a layer of hummus. This is called small scale weathering.

Sedimentary: Zones

Between the Earth's surface and her water table is the zone where many new minerals are formed due to the release of compounds and elements from water, some of which are carried to deeper locations. This occurs particularly among rocks which are rich in ore.

Due to the fact that oxygen is still available at this level, the region above the water table is called the "weathering or oxidation zone." Chemically, oxidation occurs by a release of chemicals. When this occurs with metal atoms, they transform into charged particles (ions). It is only in the form of ions that they are able to form new compounds. Some mineral s found in the oxidation zone are azurite, malachite chrysocolla, dioptase, turquoise and variscite.

The next zone is called the "cementation zone: due to a process known as cementation during which metal ions turn back into neutral metal atoms. Chemically, this process is the opposite of oxidation because neutral metal atoms do not remain in solution and they collect electrons. Among minerals typical to this zone are copper or silver, copper-chalcedony and Covellite.

To summarize the principle of Sedimentary Formation: it is a process in which the solid structures of certain rocks are dissolved through environmental influences. The mineral forming elements released through this dissolving process and other substances brought there through environmental activity create new minerals. The new minerals are known as "secondary" minerals.

Sedimentary: Healing Properties

Sedimentary Rocks and Secondary Minerals correlate directly with another aspect of our beingness in the influence of our environment.

The sedimentary formation principle is a process during which the solid structures of certain rocks are dissolved through environmental influences. This is the same process which occurs in our lives. We are shaped by the experiences of our past, particularly childhood experiences where we make decisions based on pleasurable or painful experiences. Additionally, we develop survival strategies during the early years and are also provided with "explanations" for the way we find the world. Humans will tend to take on the opinions of those people whom we most trust.

In some cases, this kind of shaping encourages development; however, very often, it happens that rigid patters we absorbed discourage development and they become useless and stand in our way at a later time. For instance, if the survival strategy we learn as children is "cry loudly and I will get whatever I want," then we shouldn't be surprised if nobody likes us much later on because we never stop moaning and crying.

Sedimentary rocks and secondary minerals make it easier for us to recognize the shaping we experience which is based on learned beliefs. By becoming more consciously aware of these learned beliefs, we can become able to release and dissolve them.

Secondary minerals also will help with new ways of looking at things and with developing more suitable strategies which are tailored to present situations. This is one way tin which our inner needs can be more easily brought into harmony with our environment. Stress and tensions are dissolved and harmony restored which brings about healing of diseases that

result from conflicts with our environment.

Metamorphic

In the depths of the Earth, the lower part of the crust between the Magma and the Sedimentary formation area, is an area where there is enormous pressure and the hot magma is always present.

The Earth's crust is not evenly thick and firm all the way around. It consists of "plates" which float on top of magma in the same way that ice floats in water. The plates vary in thickness—below the ocean (oceanic plates) they are 3 to 6 miles thick—below the land (continental plates) they are 13 to 38 miles thick. As with icebergs, only a small portion is visible at the top. The reason we have the distinct separation of oceans and dry land is that the continental plates rise up further than the oceanic plates.

Because of convection within the magma, the various plates of the Earth's crust are always in motion. During the process of their motion, the plates are pushed on top of each other which creates areas where they cross each other and become buckled or folded up. This is how mountains are formed. Note that only about 10% of the total mass is pushed upward, the remainder is pushed down.

The above processes do not occur without having an effect on the rocks involved. The rocks involved are under extreme pressure and begin to restructure themselves. Crystals, which were originally randomly joined with others, begin to organize themselves under this great pressure, generally end up crossways to the pressure and substances are then squeezed out of them. These substances then accumulate and form new, more resistant minerals which may also be combined with elements of other moving rocks which further form new minerals in a boundary layer.

This process is also assisted by heat acting upon the rocks, although with the pressure involved, the heat does not turn them in to magma or liquid form. This process is metamorphosis, the process which changes the shape and appearance of rocks and minerals.

Metamorphosis also occurs if rocks become even more compressed and heavier when they are overlaid with new layers and then they end up sinking into the depths of the Earth. This occurs in large areas and is known as regional metamorphosis. Among minerals formed this way are: crystalline slate, Kyanite, garnet, jade, nephrite, serpentine, tiger iron and zoisite. Limestone is transformed by the metamorphosis process into marble, in which deposits of lapis lazuli or emeralds can sometimes be found.

Some rocks and minerals are formed in the area of rising magma because of very high temperatures. This is called small scale metamorphosis. For instance, around a volcanic chimney are often found rubies and sapphires.

Metasomatism is the addition of new elements by migration in the rock. This occurs when there is an additional exchange of elements in surrounding rocks, many times through vapors dissolving certain elements out of rock and replacing them with others. Examples of minerals formed this way are charoite, rhodonite, falcon's eye and tiger's eye.

In summary, metamorphosis is the transformation of existing rock under the influence of heat and pressure in the interior of the Earth. The rock is not melted down, but it undergoes structure and mineral content changes, takes on a completely different shape and appearance as the transformation occurs from the inside out. This process includes severe testing of the rock because only what is unaffected by pressure and heat will be retained, everything else is transformed until a new state occurs. Minerals formed this wary or known as "tertiary" minerals.

Metamorphic: Healing Properties

Metamorphic rocks test aspects of our lives in terms of their durability, just as they were constantly tested during their formation.

Too often, we do not release the old but we hold on to it because we are comfortable with it or simply because it is known. We continue as usual, however; there is a sense of something not being right. We can ignore this sense which will result in some sort of dis-ease, or we can deal with it.

Use of tertiary minerals and metamorphic rocks will assist us with this process. When we use them, everything that is not of permanent value for us will begin to take on new shapes and forms—things will come to an end naturally without seeming to be any necessity for trauma around it.

The metamorphic formation principle represents a transformation process in which everything that cannot withstand the heat and pressure is changed into a new form from the inside out.

The head and pressure inside us may lead us through a phase of dissatisfaction in which we are very self-critical. We question everything—whether it makes sense and is of value in our lives.
We often begin a radical clean-up. This is the way we transform our lives into completely new forms.

Metamorphic rocks and tertiary minerals stimulate this inner transformation process by encouraging critical self-reflection and help us to realize and understand those things in our lives that need to end because they make us dissatisfied. They assist in bringing about radical changes which lead to a more fulfilled life—they will also assist in all matters of diseases which are rooted in the fear of letting go. By stimulating an inner transformation, they help

us to overcome attachments, habits and compromises.

LEVEL 2

COLOR PSYCHOLOGY & BALANCING THE CHAKRAS WITH COLOR

COLOR PSYCHOLOGY

Light consists of the seven color energies: Red, Orange, Yellow, Green, Blue, Indigo and Violet. Each color is connected to various areas of our body, and each affects us emotionally, physically, mentally, and spiritually. By learning how color psychology influences us, we can effectively use color therapy to give us an extra boost of energy when we need it. If you wake up in the morning with little energy, or you need to prepare for a business meeting, the power of colors can help. All you need to do is reflect on the type of day you have planned; choose the color that will help you meet the demands of the day; and then absorb that particular color. It's like fueling your system with the right kind of gas! The following is a brief description of the different colors, the color energies, and the effects of color psychology on us as humans.

Red Color: VITALITY, COURAGE, SELF CONFIDENCE
Use red when you need to meet a demanding day, when your immune system is suffering, or when you feel drained of energy. The color red provides the power from the earth and gives energy on all levels. It connects us to our physical body. All projects needs the life vitality of red at their begninngs. Red Personality Traits: Courage, confidence, humanism, strong-will, spontaneity, honesty, and extroversion. The Root Chakra is governed by the red energy.

Orange Color: HAPPINESS, CONFIDENCE, RESOURCEFULNESS
Orange brings joy to your workday and strengthens your appetite for life! Orange is the best emotional stimulant. It's a great color to bring you back to life on a dull, cloudy day. It also helps depression. It connects us to our senses and helps to remove inhibitions and makes us independent and social. Personality Traits: Enthusiasm, happiness, sociability, energy, self-assurance, and cooperation. The Spleen Chakra is governed by the orange energy.

Yellow Color: WISDOM, CLARITY, SELF-ESTEEM
Yellow gives us clarity of thought, increases our awareness, and stimulates our interest and curiosity. Yellow energy is related to the ability to perceive and understand. The yellow energy connects us to our mental self and is great for memory, studying for exams and creating confidence. Personality Traits: Good-humor, optimism, confidence, practicality, and intellectual sharpness. The solar plexus Chakra is governed by the yellow energy.

Green Color: BALANCE, LOVE, SELF CONTROL
Green helps relax muscles, nerves, and thoughts. It cleanses and balances our energy to give us a feeling of renewal, peace and harmony. Green connects us to unconditional love and is used for balancing our whole being. Excellent color to replenish when you feel emotionally drained. Personality Traits: Understanding, self-controlled, adaptable, sympathetic, compassionate, generous, humble, nature loving, and romantic. The Heart Chakra is governed by the green energy.

Blue Color: KNOWLEDGE, HEALTH, and DECISIVENESS
Blue is a mentally relaxing color. Blue has a pacifying effect on the nervous system and brings great relaxation. It is ideal for sleep problems, and hyperactive children. It connects us to holistic thought, and gives us wisdom and clarity, enhancing communication and speech. Personality Traits: Loyalty, tact, affection, inspiration, inventiveness, caring, and cautious. The Throat Chakra is governed by the blue energy.

Indigo Color: INTUITION, MYSTICISM, UNDERSTANDING
The indigo energy connects us to our unconscious self and gives us the experience of being part of the whole universe. Strengthens intuition, imagination, psychic powers, and increases

dream activity. Personality Traits: Intuition, fearlessness, practicality, idealism, wisdom, and truth seeking. The Brow Chakra is governed by the indigo energy.

Violet Color: BEAUTY, CREATIVITY, and INSPIRATION
Violet purifies our thoughts and feelings giving us inspiration in all undertakings. The violet energy connects us to our spiritual self-bringing guidance, wisdom and inner strength. Enhances artistic talent and creativity. Personality Traits: Inspirational leaders, kindly and just, humanitarians, self-scarifying, visionary, creative, and strong mentally. The Crown Chakra is governed by the violet energy.

Balancing the Chakras

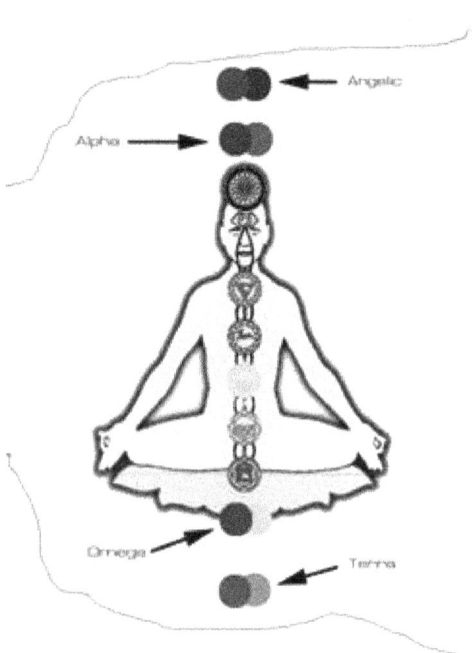

Among my own modalities are the balancing of chakras with tuning forks and the use of Crystaline Reiki.

Color is used in many forms to heal and aid the sick, diseased, and distressed. As a color therapist I use the following color to balance the eleven chakras of the physical and energy body. I always start with the heart chakra, the center of the human form and the seat of the soul.

Here are the colors I use to balance the eleven chakras:

Heart Chakra: Green (4th)
Green is the color of harmony and balance. It is good for tired nerves and it helps with the heart area. It will balance the emotions and bring about a feeling of calmness. Green is a good general healing color because it stimulates growth, so it is good for helping heal broken bones, and tissue distress of all kinds. Green is a good color for pregnant women as it helps create an atmosphere of serenity and calm. Too much green may create more negative energy if there is some already present in the person being treated.

Solar Plexus Chakra: Yellow (3rd)

Yellow is the color of intellect and it is used for mental stimulation; it will help you think with greater sharpness and clarity. It is good for clearing a foggy head. It can be used to help cure dermatitis and other skin problems, but again it must be used carefully because it is very stimulating and can possibly cause exhaustion and depression.

Throat Chakra: Blue (5th)
Blue is the color of truth, serenity, and harmony by helping to soothe the mind. Blue is good for cooling, calming, rebuilding, and protecting. Blue will help feverish conditions; it will help stop bleeding and will help with nervous irritation. It is very good for burns. Too much blue can leave you cold, depressed and sorrowful.

Sacral Chakra: Orange (2nd)
Orange is also a color of energy. It is used to increase immunity, to increase sexual potency, and to help in all digestive aliments, chest, and kidney diseases. Orange will give a gentle warming effect if used lightly. Orange, like red should not be used for too long. It is not a good color for people who are nervous or easily agitated.

Third Eye: Purple (6th)
Purple is a color that will connect you with your spiritual self. It is good for mental and nervous problems. It will assist very well with rheumatism and epilepsy. It helps with pain, is used in deep tissue work, and helps heal bones. If you use too much purple and you run the risk of detaching too much from reality!

Root Chakra: Red (1st)
Red is the color of energy, vitality, and power. It can be used to reduce pain and to warm cold areas. Red is a powerful agent for healing diseases of the blood or circulation. It will help with depression. Red should not be used on people who have high blood pressure or anxiety. If you stay under the red ray for too long or are exposed to red for a considerable time, it will make you very agitated or even aggressive.

Crown Chakra: Indigo (7th)
Indigo is a higher aspect of blue, so it will have all the attributes of blue. Additionally, indigo is very good for the head. It will clear a congested head to allow a clear path for consciousness to rise to the spiritual self. It is used for the diseases of the ears, nose, and eyes. It is also very good for sinuses. Indigo is a good astringent and it is a good purifier. Too much indigo can give you a headache and it can also make you very drowsy.

Omega Chakra: Infrared (8th)
Infrared is a more intense form of red. It helps to keep one's boundaries by protecting one from psychic and physical attack.

Alpha Chakra: Lavender (9th)
Lavender is the color of equilibrium; it helps with spiritual healing. It is used as a tranquilizer and it will aid sleep. It is a color of replenishing and rebuilding. It is like a tonic for the body. Too much will make you very tired and disoriented.

Terra Chakra: Silver (10th)
Silver is the color of peace and persistence. It is the major purging color so it is very good for removing unwanted diseases and troubles from the body.

Angelica Chakra: Gold (11th)

Gold is the strongest color to help cure all illnesses. Gold strengthens all fields of the body and spirit.

SACRED HEALING SPACE

The sacred healing space begins with the Gate of Grace, an opening of a space in which an atmosphere of stable healing can exist undisturbed. In this space, a ball of Grace forms to allow for healing and communication with the angelic realm. This space increases the healing of any modality used inside the Sacred Healing Space. To increase the power of this Sacred Space surrounds the Space with an Aurauralite Grid.

This is how it works. Once you have the stones in place, they allow two four-sided pyramids to form. One pyramid points upward and the other points down into the ground.

The bases of each are a quarter turn from each other; from a 2-dimensional top view, they form an eight-pointed star shape. Three dimensionally, they form what is called a Star Octahedron, with the points of the base of the downward pointing pyramid sticking out through the sides of the upward pointing pyramid and the points of the base of the upward pointing pyramid sticking out through the sides of the downward pointing pyramid.

The upward pointing pyramid will start to turn clockwise and the downward pointing pyramid will turn counter clockwise. As they begin to spin faster, the points on the bases passing through the sides will start to make facets. These facets reflect the energy back inwards creating a ball shape as the energy bounces back and forth from top and bottom opening a vortex, or torus tube, through which the breath of God flows.

I have found it a good idea to leave the area while the Sacred Healing Space/Gate of Grace stablizes itself. Some people have experienced dizziness and slight pressure in their foreheads by staying close to the Sacred Healing Space before it stabilizes. The Stabilization process takes about an hour to complete. Once the Sacred Healing Space is open and stable you may return without these side effects. People that are sensitive to enrgy can feel the energy of the Sacred Healing Space from about 15 to 20 feet away as they return.

The energy that flows through the Sacred Healing Space is Grace. Of course, Grace is already everywhere all the time. However, in the Sacred Healing Space, it is completely free flowing and unobstructed. This allows healing to take place with whatever healing modality one chooses to use.

Given that it is also used for communication with the angelic realm, people have gotten answers to questions they have been looking for; some by finally "just knowing" and others by actually hearing the nasers. Whichever way they get the answers, they are clearer than ever before as to the way they will go in their life's work. To each person comes a sense of peace and knowing that everything is going to work out. There is a down side to this as some people have tried to sleep in the Sacred healing Space. I do not suggest someone try this because you don't get much sleep. While in the Sacred Healing Space you are receiving information. This interferes with one's sleep cycle and they do not get the sleep they need. At least this what has been reported to Joe Crain, and myself by those who have set it up around beds.

You should remember that the Sacred Healing Space is on Holy ground. This is a gift for all of us to use and not a plaything. If someone should try to use it for things it was not meant for it will shut down, just like an Aurauralite Power Stone Grid. It can't be used to hurt anyone or make things happen. The most powerful use of the Sacred Healing Space comes from love. When the love you bring to the Sacred Healing Space is mixed with love that God is, all things are possible. Teach only love.

Setting up the Sacred Healing Space

In order to set up the Sacred Healing Space you will need a few things such as a thirty-foot measuring tape, eight stones, eight push-pins (for pinning the stones to the ceiling as I have done). The layout the can be large and outside or smaller and inside as I have done mine in the healing room (12 X12) for the larger Sacred Healing Space eight length of wood (Joe Crain used 4X4 posts to set his outside space), then follow the following Diagrams, A, B, C, D, and E, to set your sacred healing space.

*The Sacred Healing Space was given to Dr. Joe Crain from Arch Angel Michael, during one of Michael's many visits to Dr. Joe Crain. The above information is used with permission from Dr. Joe Crain.

Diagram A

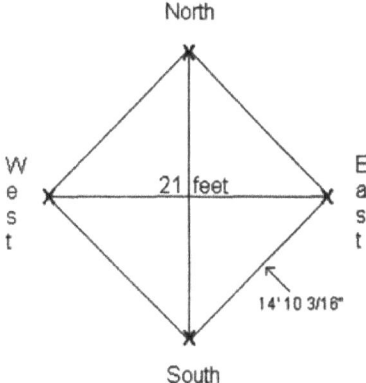

Find a center point and measure from that point 10 1/2 feet North, 10 1/2 feet South, 10 1/2 feet East and 10 1/2 feet West. Mark the 4 end points. The total distance from the north and south endpoints will be 21 feet and the total distance from the west and east endpoints will be 21 feet. It is important that the lines in the diagram are measured exactly perpendicular (at right angles). When laying out the design, it is helpful to use long pieces of string tied to the endpoints and crossing at the center. This will help to eyeball if the lines are running at right angles. As a double check on the placement, the diagonal distance between each of the points should be approximately 14 feet 10 and 3/16 inches.

Diagram B

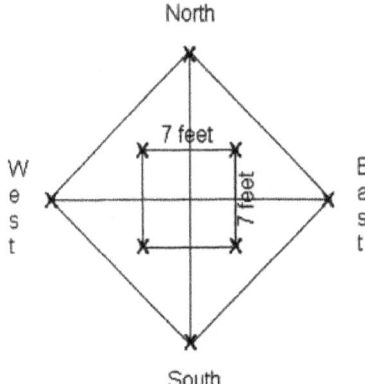

From the center point, measure 3 1/2 feet north, then 3 1/2 feet east, mark the point. Then measure 7 feet south and mark the point, then 7 feet west and mark the point, then 7 feet north and mark the point. If the points were connected, this would form a square with 4 equal sides of 7 feet.

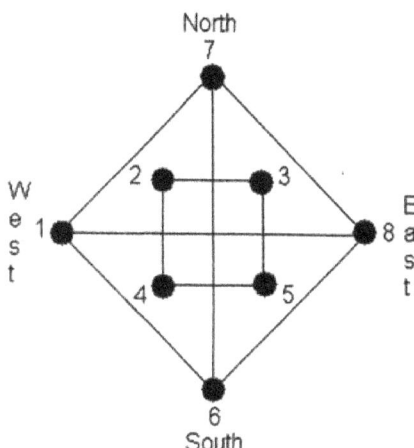

Diagram C

Set a post in the ground at each of the eight points you have marked. The posts should be made of wood only. A 4 x 4 works well, you can also use a 2 X 2 or a dowel rod. Each post should be the following height **from the ground:**

1) 7"   West
2) 14"   Northwest
3) 21"   Northeast
4) 24 1/2" Southwest
5) 31 1/2" Southeast
6) 38 1/2" South
7) 45 1/2" North
8) 7"   East

These posts need to be below the ground far enough to support its height. All posts with a height of 24 1/2" and smaller should have at least 12" under the ground and all posts with a height greater than 24 1/2" should have at least 18" under the ground.

Diagram D

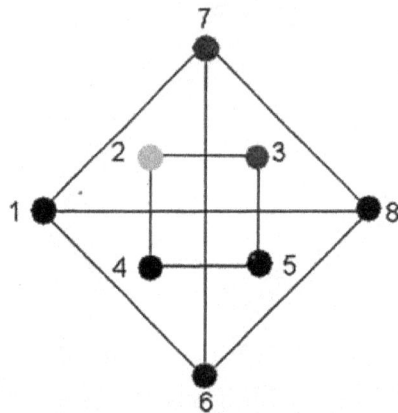

Place the appropriate stones on top of each of the posts as follows (each stone represents a musical note color and church and that is listed here as well):

	Note	Scale	Color	Church	Crystal or Stone
1)	C	do	Blue	Philadelphia	Blue sapphire or azurite or blue aventurine
2)	D	re	Yellow	Pergamum	Yellow sapphire or yellow topaz or yellow calcite
3)	E	me	Orange	Ephesus	Orange calcite or orange sapphire or carnelian
4)	F	fa	Purple	Thyatira	Amethyst or benitoite
5)	G	so	Red	Smyrna	Ruby crystal or jewel
6)	A	la	Green	Sardis	Emerald or kyanite or fluorite
7)	B	te	Violet	Laodicea	Lavender jade or violet calcite or charoite
8)	C	do	Blue	Philadelphia	Blue sapphire or azurite or blue aventurine

Diagram E

This is the final design of the Gate of Grace.

AURAURALITE POWER STONE GRID

Grids should be placed inside the healing room or area where the healing will be taking place. To set up a 5 stone Power Grid, place a stone in each corner of the room and one in the center of the room. Once the four corner stones are in place, hold the 5th stone or center rock and give the grid the following command- "I set this grid in place to enhance the sacred healing space so that it may provide healing for all those that enter this space, and that the healing be for the highest good". The tell the grid to "turn on" as you place the center stone. You can instantly feel it charging up and creating an energy of stability and clarity.

LEVEL 3

A BRIEF HISTORY OF TUNING FORKS

1711, England, Royal trumpeter and flutiest, John Shore, created the first tuning fork, it was made of steel.

1800, German physicist E.F.F. Chladni, along with others, constructed a complete musical instrument based on sets of tuning forks.

1834, J.H. Scheibler presented a set of 54 tuning forks covering ranges from 220 Hz to 440Hz.

1863 in Heidelberg, physiologist H. Helmholtz, used sets of electro magnetically powered tuning forks for his experiments on the sensations of tone.

1960s the Swiss scientist Hans Jenny discovered that low frequency sounds produced simple geometric shapes and as the sound frequency increased, the shapes became more complex. He also found that the sound 'OH' produced a perfect circle and that the sound, 'OM' produced a pattern similar to that of the ancient Indian mandala for 'OM'.

1974, a professional jazz musician, Fabien Maman, noticed that by playing certain musical notes that he could have an energizing effect on the audience.

1974 John Beaulieu discovered that tuning forks could be used to tune the human nervous system while working at Bellevue Psychiatric Hospital in New York City under a research grant from New York University. After over five hundred hours of listening to my nervous system, I suddenly realized that the nervous system could be "tuned like a musical instrument"

1978, Fabien joined with the senior researcher at the National Centre for Scientific Research in Paris, Helen Grimal, to study the effects of sound on normal and malignant cells.

1980, Barbara Hero studies sound frequencies on the Organs and how each Organ has a specific frequency.

1982, formation of the Sound Healers Association, by Jonathan Goldman

1988, Dr. Robert Girard used the frequency of 528 Hz to repair DNA.

1988, Dr. David Hulse, rediscovers the ancient Solfeggio Frequencies, through in his research, by reading the book "The Healing Codes of Biological Apocalypse" by Dr. Leonard Horowitz.

1988, Anne Christine Tooley begins research on tuning fork frequencies and discovers many things and creates a company, Luminanti Inc., which sells tuning forks. Anne's research included; a sharps set, an endocrine/spine set, kabbalah sets, and a periodic table set.

1995 Dr. Joe Crain creates Acutuning, a method for using tuning forks in the healing process.

1997- Charles Lightwalker begins research on sound healing with tuning forks using various frequencies to open the psychic pathways and enhance intuitive abilities and to develop ways of harmonizing the Endocrine system the lymphatic system and combining the various tuning fork methods into a multi level healing modality.

2008- International Tuning Fork Research Alliance created by Dr. Larry Pannell, Charles Lightwalker, Dr. Helene Pelissier, Dr. Rick Boatright, John Beaulieu, ND, PhD, Jan Longshore M.S., massage therapist & instructor Sandy Singh (all from the USA) along with Dr.Aminu Kazeem Olawale from Nigeria, Huang Yuanzhong from China, and Jan Morgans from the United Kingdom to peruse the continued research into the use of tuning forks in the healing process.

HERE ARE SOME REFERENCES:

Dr. Tomatis used high frequency sounds (3,000Hz and above) to activate the brain and affect cognitive functions such as thinking, spatial perception, and memory. Listening to these sounds increased attentiveness and concentration.

Sound therapist Jonathan Goldman in his book, *Healing Sounds*, states that frequency plus Intention equal Healing.

In her book, *The Use of Tuning Forks in Vibratory Energy Application* by Diane Hesse, Hesse describes various use of tuning fork in the application of healing.

Sound Healing with Tuning Forks Handbook By Charles/Lightwalker
This book is a general overview of healing with tuning forks and covers balancing the chakras and harmonizing the Organs.

Sound Healing with Tuning Forks Manual By Charles Lightwalker
This manual is used in the certification workshop "Tuning Fork Intensive" and covers the process used by "Certified Tuning Fork Practitioners" to balance the chakras, Harmonize the Organs, Enhance Stems Cells, Pain Relief, the Endocrine and Lymphatic Systems, and Opening the Psychic Pathways.

In his book *Crystaline Reiki: A New Frequency of Healing*, Dr. Charles Lightwalker use tuning forks combined with Reiki to create a powerful healing experience.

The book *Intuitive Emotional Release* by Dr. Charles Lightwalker use tuning forks combined with bodywork to create a dynamic release process that release stuck emotions and traumas.

The research continues on this healing modality, Tuning forks, and will show the advances that using tuning forks can have on the effect of disease and illness on the human form.

Tuning fork can be sued with so many other healing modalities, Massage, Reiki, Quantum Touch, Aromatherapy, Bodywork, Trager, Healing Touch, Spiritual Healing, Chiropractic, Acupuncture, and many others.

SELECTING AND USING A TUNING FORK

A tuning fork is a precision-made instrument designed to produce a single frequency. There are three primary considerations when selecting a fork, the type of metal, weighted vs. un-weighted and frequency.

ALUMINUM VS. STEEL

The most common metals used are aluminum and steel. Based on my experience, I recommend and offer aluminum tuning forks. Aluminum is lighter than steel, important if you will be treating clients. Another characteristic is that aluminum tends to hold the vibration longer; the sound produced by steel fades more quickly. While aluminum and steel are the most common metals, many people in the healing arts will request tuning forks that contain certain metals such as gold, silver, or platinum. This is purely a personal preference.

WEIGHTED VS. UN-WEIGHTED

Selecting weighted vs. un-weighted tuning forks has more to do with application than preference. Weighted Tuning Forks Weighted tuning forks have a round weight at the end of each prong. The weight creates a deeper vibration making it very useful for acupuncturists, chiropractors, massage therapists, cranial sacral practitioners, and energy workers. Placing the stem of a weighted fork on the body creates a deep vibration which clients often find relaxing and soothing. Most weighted forks will promote this state, however, the 128hz and/or the Om fork, 136.1hz are highly recommended for this purpose. The deep, soothing vibrations of these forks help to relax muscles, tendons, joints, and the nervous system. This occurs due to the release of nitric oxide into our system. When the body is relaxed, it is more receptive to healing. Chiropractic adjustments are often easier when the stem of the 128 is placed along the area to be adjusted. Acupuncturists will use the stem of the 128 along meridians and on acupuncture points to stimulate the body.

Cranial sacral practitioners massage therapists and energy workers will use the 128hz and 136.1hz along the body or by the ears before a session to promote a relaxed state for themselves and their client.

UN-WEIGHTED TUNING FORKS

As the name suggests, un-weighted forks do not have a weight on the prongs. These are most often used around the body and by the ears for spiritual or emotional therapy. They can be tapped individually and placed by the ears or tapped together to create harmonics. It is also recommended that you try holding several forks in one hand with one in the other, tapping several together creating what Dr. Beaulieu calls a "sonic massage." When done with the Solfeggio set, the client can be eased into an extremely deep and silent meditative state.

STANDARD OR WEIGHTED?

Standard tuning forks are great for vibrational healing such as sound toning, and for working with energies, such as opening energy blocks, clearing chakras, or cleansing auras. In the process of promoting the flow of vital life force within the human body and the human energy field, they are intended to assist and facilitate clearing, balancing, and energizing the energy body in a simple and gentle way. Standard tuning forks also have the unique quality of being able to produce harmonic intervals (multiple pitches that occur at the same time) when struck together.

Weighted tuning forks don't produce harmonic intervals as easily, however they have a much stronger vibration, making them easier to feel, and excellent for uses such as acupuncture, sound puncture, and muscle relaxation techniques. In addition to their own sound and vibrational healing qualities, weighted tuning forks can physically transfer their frequency of vibration to the body by using forced resonance, or by directly applying the handle (also called stem) of the tuning fork on the body at point of focus, such as a meridian or chakra. This is a way of creating movement or frequency vibration in any area of the body, and as such, weighted tuning forks are known to give immediate relief from pain when used with interferential therapy techniques. Weighted tuning forks vibrate for longer periods of time, and stay at their exact frequency longer. This makes them great for accurate or precision tuning or toning when doing sessions on yourself or others.

HEALING WITH TUNING FORKS

Tuning forks enhance the ability to heal and make profound changes in the energy levels of the body using sound. Tuning forks are used to correct imbalances, uncover emotions, stimulate growth, development growth and transformation and facilitate inner harmony and wholeness.

The sound waves of the Forks vibrate and travel deeply into the body along energy pathways, effecting human physiology and reaching places not easily accessed by traditional medicine. Applying the Forks stimulates and balances the body's physical and subtle energy field to promote healing and inner harmony.

Vibrational Measurement:
   A vibration is measured by how frequently it happens on a given scale, or by its frequency.
   The common unit of measurement is referred to as Hertz (named after Heninrich Rudolph Hertz). One hertz (abbreviated Hz) is one vibration, or one cycle of vibration per second.

What is Resonance?
   Resonance is the act of creating, adding, or intensifying vibration, including sound vibration by allowing one object to interact with another.
   For example using the heart chakra tuning fork on the heart chakra, it will cause the chakra to resonate sympathetically, bringing the chakra into balance.

Healing Through Sound Therapy/Healing
   When an organ, gland, chakra or body part is healthy, it creates a natural resonant frequency in harmony with the rest of the body. When the vibration of an organ, chakra or body part is out of harmony we have disease.
   Disease creates a different vibrational frequency in the affected part of the body, chakra or organ. When the correct vibrational frequency is directed into the diseased area, correct harmonic balance is restored.

   Sound Healing is effective in assisting energetic integration in a variety of healing modalities such as:
- Aromatherapy
- Acupuncture
- Chiropractic
- Hypnotherapy
- Massage

- Reiki
- Spiritual healing
- Therapeutic Touch
- Crystal & Gemstone Healing

BALANCING THE CHAKRAS & THE ORGANS

An assumption is being made that anyone using this manual already possesses an understanding of the Chakra System. A more in-depth presentation on the glands and various states of physical dysfunction associated with each chakra is beyond the scope of this manual. Many fine books are in circulation that contains in-depth presentations of each chakra.

The chakras, the body's energy centers, can be thought of as being a series of steps or lessons one must learn as they ascend from the physical level to the Divine level. Carolyn Myss, in her book "Anatomy of the Spirit," says that each chakra is the center for a particular power. These powers ascend from the densest physical power to the most spiritual power. She states that these powers seem to match the challenges we face in our lives. Each chakra is also associated with various glands and functions of the body.

The standard set of tuning forks can be used in many ways when the characteristics, glands, and powers of each chakra are considered. They may be used to enhance meditation on each chakra, clear out old patterns, release blockages, clear out congestion, physical dysfunctions, and raise our vibratory level to help our efforts to work through or with any of the challenges the chakras represent.

Following are just a few of the many characteristics, issues, emotions, mental areas, and glands in which tuning forks might be of value. The more one knows about the positive and negative attributes or characteristics of the chakra system, the more versatile the tuning forks become.

THE ELEVEN-CHAKRA SYSTEM
A Brief Outline by Sherry Fields

The human body contains hundreds of locations where there is focused and concentrated energy. There are, however, twelve major energy centers, commonly referred to as "chakras." Chakra is a Sanskrit word, which means, "wheel." The chakras are similar to wheels in that they are spinning vortexes of energy. They are centers of force located within our etheric body, through which we receive, transmit, and process life energies.

Eastern philosophy has taught a system based on seven chakras for thousands of years and is the basis for spiritual growth in many cultures. Today the angelic realms are teaching a Twelve Chakra system based on lost and forgotten information that will serve as tools to assist humanity in its spiritual journey.

Each chakra in the body is recognized as a focal point for life-force relating to spiritual, physical, emotional, and mental energies. The chakras are the network through which the mind, body, and spirit interact as one holistic system. These major chakras correspond to specific aspects of our consciousness and have their own individual characteristics and functions. Most have a corresponding relationship to one of the various glands of the body's endocrine system, as well as to colors of the rainbow spectrum.

The main purpose in working with and understanding the chakras is to create integration and wholeness within ourselves. In this way, we bring the various aspects of our consciousness from the physical to the spiritual, into a harmonious relationship. Ultimately, we begin to recognize that the various aspects of ourselves all work together, and that each aspect is as much a part of the whole as the others. We must be able to acknowledge, integrate, and accept all levels of our being.

To help us in the process of our unfolding it is most important to understand that the chakras are doorways for our consciousness. They are the doorways through which emotional, mental, and spiritual force flow into physical _expression. They are openings through which our attitudes and belief systems enter into and create our mind/ body structure. The energy created from our emotional and mental attitudes runs though the chakras and is distributed to our cells, tissues, and organs. Realizing this brings tremendous insight into how we ourselves affect our bodies, minds, and circumstances for better or for worse. To understand the chakras and their relationship to our consciousness is to better understand ourselves. Understanding ourselves will enable us to make our choices and decisions from a place of balance and awareness, rather than being blindly influenced by forces we do not understand.

This outline is a brief description only. For more comprehensive information on the first seven chakras please refer to the many books on the subject. Two good ones are "The Energy of Anatomy" by Carolyn Myss and "The Wheels of Life" by Anodea Judith.

FIRST CHAKRA: ROOT or BASE CHAKRA
Location: Base of the spine (coccyx)
Color: Red (secondary color is black)
Element: Earth
Functions: Gives vitality to the physical body. Life-force survival, self-preservation, instincts survival. Relationship to our tribe, our community, and our family.
Glands /organs: Adrenals, kidneys, spinal column, leg bones.
Gems /minerals: Ruby, garnet, bloodstone, red jasper, black tourmaline, obsidian, and smoky quartz.
Foods: Proteins, Red fruits and vegetables.
Associated aromas: Cedar, Clove
Sensory function: Smell
Qualities /lessons: Matters relating to the material world, success. The physical body, mastery of the body. Grounding, individuality, stability, security, stillness, health, courage, and patience.
Negative qualities: Self-centered, insecurity, violence, greed, and anger.

SECOND CHAKRA: SPLEEN CHAKRA (Sacral Plexus)
Location: Lower abdomen to navel area
Color: Orange
Element: Water
Functions: Procreation, assimilation of food, physical force and vitality, sexuality.
Glands /organs: Ovaries, testicles, prostrate gland, genitals, spleen, womb, and bladder.
Gems /Minerals: Carnelian, coral, gold calcite, amber, citrine, gold topaz, and peach aventurine.
Foods: Liquids: Orange fruits and vegetables.
Associated aromas: Ylang/Ylang, Sandalwood
Sensory function: Taste

Qualities/lessons: Giving & receiving emotions, desire, pleasure, sexual /passionate love, change, movement, assimilation of new ideas. Health, family tolerance, and surrender. Working harmoniously and creatively with others.

Negative qualities: Overindulgence in food or sex, sexual difficulties, confusion, purposelessness, jealousy, envy, desire to possess, emotionalism.

THIRD CHAKRA: SOLAR PLEXUS

Location: Below the breastbone and behind the stomach.
Color: Golden Yellow.
Element: Fire
Functions: It is the center of personal power, ambition, intellect, astral force, desire, and emotions based on intellect and touch.
Glands/organs: Pancreas, liver, digestive tract, stomach, Liver, spleen, gall bladder, autonomic nervous system.
Gems/minerals: Tiger's Eye, Amber, Yellow Topaz, and Citrine.
Foods: Complex Carbohydrates, and Grains.
Associated aromas: Lavender, Rosemary, and Bergamot.
Sensor- function: Sight.
Qualities/lessons: Transforming. Shaping, Purifying, Shaping of Being, Mental Energy.
Negative qualities: Perfectionism, control over self versus others, self-critical thoughts, frustration, anxiety.

FOURTH CHAKRA: HEART CHAKRA

Location: Center of chest, at level of heart.
Color: Green (secondary color is pink).
Element: Air.
Functions: It is the center, which vitalizes the heart, thymus, circulatory system, blood, cellular structure, and involuntary muscles.
Glands/organs: Heart, ribs, chest cavity, lower lungs, and blood, circulatory system, skin, hands, and thymus.
Gems/minerals: Kunzite, emerald, green jade, rose quartz, and pink tourmaline.
Foods: Green vegetables, dark leafy greens.
Associated aromas: Rose oil.
Sensory function: Touch.
Qualities/lessons: The center of compassion, love, group consciousness, and spirituality associated with "oneness" with "all that is." It provides for desegregation between the loving energy of the heart and the analytical energy of the intellect. God connection. Able to give and receive. Open to change and new ideas. Coping with loss. Balance.
Negative qualities: Self-abandonment, fear, sadness, anger, resentment, jealousy, and hostility.

FIFTH CHAKRA: THROAT CHAKRA

Location: Neck, throat area above collarbone.
Color: Blue
Element: The higher _expression of all signs.
Functions: Communication center, acting to provide the energy for, and the understanding of, both verbal and mental communications.
Glands/Organs: Thyroid gland, throat and jaw areas, alimentary canal, lungs, vocal cords, and the breath.
Gems/minerals: Aquamarine, Turquoise, Chalcedony, Chrysocolla.
Foods: Fruit.
Associated aromas: Sage, eucalyptus.

Sensory function: Hearing.
Qualities/lessons: The gateway to the Higher Consciousness and the gateway through which the emotions contained on the heart must pass to become balanced and harmonized. Open, clear communication of feelings and thoughts. Creativity, speaking up, releasing, and healing.
Negative qualities: Uptight, low self-esteem, low self-confidence, hostility, anger, and resentment.

SIXTH CHAKR.A: THIRD EYE (BROW CHAKRA)
Location: Between and about one finger-breadth above the eyebrows.
Color: Indigo
Element: The higher _expression of all signs.
Functions: The center of psychic power, higher intuition, the energies of the spirit, Magnetic forces, and light. Clairvoyance, healing addictions. Central Nervous system.
Gems/minerals: Lapis lazuli, indigo, sapphire, sodalite.
Foods: Chlorophyll, breath, and air.
Associated aromas: Mint, jasmine.
Sensory function: all, inclusive ESP.
Qualities/lessons: Higher consciousness, emotional and spiritual love center, Spiritual inner sight, clairvoyance. When balanced, the mind (right hemisphere) and brain (left hemisphere) function in a Unified field. Insight ensues and its practical application becomes a daily occurrence. It also assists in the purification of negative tendencies and in the elimination of selfish attitudes.
Negative qualities: Worry, hysteria, stress, fear, shock, irritation, depression, headaches, speech and weight problems.

SEVENTH CHAKRA: CROWN CHAKRA
Location: Crown of head.
Color: Violet.
Element: The higher _expression of all elements.
Function: The center of spirituality, enlightenment, dynamic thought and energy. It is the center that vitalizes the cerebrum, the right eye, and the pineal gland.
Glands/organs: Pineal gland, cerebrum.
Gems/minerals: Amethyst, quartz crystal.
Foods: Sun, juice, fasting.
Associated aromas: Galbanum, lotus.
Sensory function: None
Qualities/lessons: It allows for the inward flow of wisdom from the ethers and brings the gift of cosmic consciousness. When stimulated and clear, it enables one to see the truth concerning illusory ideals, materialistic pursuits, self-limiting concepts, pride, and vanity; it further allows one to experience continuous self-awareness and conscious detachment from personal emotions, compassion, seeing self in others, peacefulness, oneness.
Negative qualities: Confusion, anxiety, stress.

Additional Chakras as described by Metatron:

EIGHTH CHAKRA - INFRA RED – OMEGA
Location: Midway between the root chakra and the knees
Color: Infrared, a combination of red and blue
Function: An energy transference chakra. It takes in energy from the world and other people, plants and animals and operates like a step-down or step-up transformer. Seeing the whole body and the Chakras as an integrated energy system, the Omega transfers

energy from outside the body to inside increasing or decreasing it as necessary to stimulate energy flow and release blocks.

Qualities/lessons: It is also like a two-way valve, we can use the Omega to release stored/stagnant Chi or energy, or for clearing a block/learning the lesson. Used to release also when we ask the angels/spirit to assist us to transmute negative thoughts and belief systems, past words, actions or deeds.

Negative qualities: Inactivity/sloth, emotionalism - empathic abilities run riot, getting into other people's stuff and not focusing on self growth.

NINTH CHAKRA - ULTRA VIOLET – ALPHA

Location: Between 12 and 18 inches out from the top of the head.

Color: Ultra Violet - blue and violet

Function: This chakra is the access to information about Karma, lessons, our learning abilities, doorways to dimensions and times as well as the Akashic records. When we access past life information it is through this chakra. Occasionally we can access this information in the dream state, when there is important information to be communicated to us. Often spirit/angels will use this tool to get our attention. The dream state many times expresses ideas in symbols and it is our job to interpret the symbols presented. We can of course gain confirmation of our interpretation through meditation. But first the idea or lesson must be accessed.

Qualities/lessons: Innate knowledge of the law of Karma, other dimensions and Akashic records, past life interpretation

Negative qualities: Too much reliance on outside guidance, looses communication with the higher self within.

TENTH CHAKRA - SILVER – TERRA

Location: Midway between the knees and the feet.

Color: Silver

Function: The Grounding Chakra, a receptive energy with a positive flow containing the elements of wind, earth, water and fire. It is the anchor to the physical world. We are spiritual beings having a physical experience. We need to stay balanced, emotionally, mentally, physically and spiritually.

Equally the chakras must be balanced. We are not just to work on the spiritual or upper chakras, but all of them equally. We are here in the physical for a purpose to learn and grow through the experience. It is through the Terra Chakra that we ground and connect to the earth (Gaia). This is where our sense of knowing 'nature' develops and understanding the naturalness of the cycles of life. Birth, growth then death. It is repeated everywhere in nature, in the plant life, the animal life, the mineral life even in the cosmos.

Qualities/lessons: Keeping balance here helps us to stay grounded and understand the nature of our life, the cycles and the patterns within it. It allows us to develop our natural knowing.

Negative qualities: In the unbalanced, ungrounded state we develop fears about the cycles of life, loose connection with our spiritual knowing.

ELEVENTH CHAKRA - GOLD – ANGELIC

Location: Between 18 and 24 inches out from the top of our head

Color: Gold

Function: The angelic chakra contains the programming of the soul for this lifetime and the history of the soul. It is through our connection and understanding of this chakra that we gain or affect our own healings, insights, learn our lessons, understand the soul contracts and begin to understand our life purpose.

Qualities/lessons: As we continue to evolve as physical/spiritual beings our understanding of this chakra is strengthened. We can begin to see (re-remember) the achieve those goals by living our life in the flow of its purpose instead of against it.

Negative Qualities: None, communication from the angelic realm cannot be negative.

Organs

Just like a symphony orchestra, when the organs are all in balance and healthy they sing a harmonic song of wholeness. But when one or more organ is out of balance or diseased they create a dis-functoning system effecting the other organs. By using the Organ Tuning Fork Set, one can retune the organs back into balance creating a synergistic healthy flow of life force energy. This chapter explains the process and procedure necessary to retune or rebalance the organs into a normal healthy function.

The set has 14 forks, one for each of the major organs and essential parts of the physical body. These forks are tuned to the frequencies of healthy human tissue. They can be used to elevate the body to a balanced state of health. They most efficient used in conjunction with the chakra forks in healing, but can also be used individually for a specific issue. To bring the body into alignment, balance the chakras first & then use the Organ Tuning Fork Set to correct the frequency of each organ.

The human body uses its organs to support it in staying balanced. For example if the lungs are not operating at the level of efficiency that they were meant to be, the oxygen to the rest of the body is lessened. From this the rest of the body does not have what it needs to operate correctly. When we can change the way an organ is functioning, we can get the body back into balance. To assist you in retuning the organs find listed the organs and the fork(s) to use in the process. Tap the tuning fork to get it vibrating and place the stem on or over the organ until it stops vibrating. This will assist in releasing stagnant energy, which isn't serving the organ well. Then to put energy into the organ turn the fork the other way around so that the stem is facing away from the organ.

Another way to retune the organs is by applying the tuning forks to the reflex points on the bottom of the feet. This is great if there are some difficult areas to reach. The client doesn't need to undress for the processes - you can just have him/her remove shoes and socks.

The Organs Tuning Fork Set is considered an advance set, and can be used to balance certain organs or to clear a specific emotions or issues. Using a specific Organ tuning fork to clear a specific emotion or issue can be more direct and save time when used with other healing modalities. Find below a list of the organs & their corresponding note, frequency and relevant emotions or thoughts which could create imbalance.

Blood - E 321.9 Hz. Lack of Joy.
Adrenals - B 492.8 Hz. Anxiety.
Kidneys - Eb 319.88 Hz. Fear, disappointment, failure.
Liver - Eb 317.83 Hz. Anger.
Bladder - F 352 Hz. Anxiety, fear of letting go.
Intestines - C# 281 Hz. Assimilation & absorption.
Lungs - A 220 Hz. Grief, depression, unworthy.
Colon - F 176 Hz. Releasing the past.
Gall Bladder - E 164.3 Hz. Pride, hard thoughts.
Pancreas - C# 117.3 Hz. Deep sorrow, a need to control.
Stomach - A 110 Hz. Fear of the new, dread.

Brain - Eb 315.8 Hz. Stubborn, fear, self criticism, refusing to change.
Muscles - E 324 Hz. Resistance to new experiences.

Adrenals Tuning Fork

This fork is to bring balance to the adrenals, and is tuned to the frequencies of a healthy adrenal gland. It can be used to elevate the adrenals to a balanced state of health. Strike the fork on a rubber hockey puck to get it vibrating then wave the fork over the area of the adrenals for 20 seconds. Repeat the process again for another 20 seconds.

Bladder Tuning Fork

This fork is to bring balance to the Bladder, and is tuned to the frequencies of a healthy Bladder. It can be used to elevate the bladder to a balanced state of health. Strike the fork on a rubber hockey puck, then wave the tuning fork over the Bladder area, this will bring the Bladder into balance.

Blood Tuning Fork

This fork is to bring balance to the blood system, and is tuned to the frequencies of a healthy blood system. It can be used to elevate the blood to a balanced state of health. Strike the fork on a rubber hockey puck, then while vibrating place the fork 8 inches above the heart area, waving the fork for 20 seconds. This will send the vibrational frequency into the blood stream creating a healthy flow of blood.

Brain Tuning Fork

The brain takes on external stimuli through the sensory system. Touch, taste, smell, sight and sound are all transmitted to the brain, however the connections that allow brain cells to process this information will become distorted if lacking the proper stimulation. Sensory deprivation has a significant impact on the brain.

Balancing the Sides of the Brain
- Stand at the head of the healing table facing the person lying on the table face up.
- Tap the Brain fork to start it vibrating, then place the fork with the stem placed on the right side of the temple for 20 seconds. Then repeat the process on the left temple, for 20 seconds.
- Tap the fork again and move the fork to above the ears (in the small indentation), tap the fork again and do the other side (above the ear) for 20 seconds.
- Tap again and place the stem in the small indentation behind the ear lobe. Repeat to other ear.
- Next tap again and place the stem of the brain fork on the crown of the head.
- Then use the Om fork by placing the Om fork (when vibrating) 4 inches from the ear for 20 seconds, the repeat the process on the other ear.
- This will bring the brain organ back into a balanced frequency.

Colon Tuning Fork

This fork is to bring balance to the colon, and is tuned to the frequencies of healthy colon. It can be used to elevate the organ to a balanced state of health. Strike the fork on a rubber hockey puck, once the fork is vibrating wave the fork over the colon area for 20 seconds, this will bring the colon into harmonic balance.

Gall Bladder Tuning Fork

This fork is to bring balance to the Gall Bladder, and is tuned to the frequencies of a healthy Gall Bladder. It can be used to elevate the Gall Bladder to a balanced state of health. Strike the fork on a rubber hockey puck, once the fork is vibrating wave the fork over the Gall Bladder area for 20 seconds, this will bring the Gall Bladder into harmonic balance.

Intestines Tuning Fork

This fork is part of the Organ Tuning Forks Set. This fork is to bring balance to the Intestines, and is tuned to the frequencies of healthy Intestines. It can be used to elevate the Intestines to a balanced state of health. Strike the fork on a rubber hockey puck, once the fork is vibrating wave the fork over the Gall Bladder area for 20 seconds, this will bring the Gall Bladder into harmonic balance.

Kidneys Tuning Fork

This fork is to bring balance to the kidneys, and is tuned to the frequencies of healthy kidneys. It can be used to elevate the kidneys to a balanced state of health. Strike the tuning fork on a rubber hockey puck, once the tuning fork is vibrating wave the tuning fork over the Kidney area, this will bring the Kidney into balance.

Liver Tuning Fork

This fork is to bring balance to the liver, and is tuned to the frequencies of healthy liver tissue. It can be used to elevate the liver to a balanced state of health. Use the Liver tuning fork by striking the fork on a rubber hockey puck, once the tuning fork is vibrating, wave the tuning fork over the Liver area, this will bring the Liver into balance.

Lungs Tuning Fork

This fork is to bring balance to the Lungs, and is tuned to the frequencies of healthy Lungs. It can be used to elevate the Lungs to a balanced state of health. Use the Lung tuning forks by striking it on a rubber hockey puck, once the fork is vibrating wave the fork over the lungs over 20 seconds, this will bring the Lungs into balance.

Muscles Tuning Fork

This fork is to bring balance to the Muscles, and is tuned to the frequencies of healthy Muscles. It can be used to elevate the Muscles to a balanced state of health.
Use the Muscles tuning fork by striking it on a rubber hockey puck, once the fork is vibrating wave the fork over the Muscles of the body (especially over muscles that are sore, strained or injured), this would bring the Muscles into balance.

Pancreas Tuning Fork

This fork is to bring balance to the Pancreas, and is tuned to the frequencies of a healthy Pancreas. It can be used to elevate the Pancreas to a balanced state of health.

Stomach Tuning Fork

This fork is to bring balance to the stomach, and is tuned to the frequencies of healthy stomach tissue. It can be used to elevate the stomach to a balanced state of health. Use the Stomach tuning fork by striking it on a rubber hockey puck, once the fork is vibrating wave the fork over the stomach area for 20 seconds, this will bring the Stomach into balance.

USING TUNING FORKS ALONGSIDE CRYSTALS & GEMSTONES

The following information is on the use of tuning forks with Crystals and Gemstones in the healing process.

First relax your client with the Om fork while they lay on the healing table then, balance the chakras by placing stones on the chakra area and then use the tuning forks over these same areas, waving the fork over the stone and chakra 3 times for 20 seconds each. Begin with the heart chakra, and then move to the third chakra, then the fifth chakra, then the second chakra, then the sixth chakra, then the first chakra, then seventh chakra, then the Omega chakra, then the alpha chakra, then the terra chakra then the angelic chakra, then seal in the balancing with the creation fork.

Next move on to the Organs, and bring them into harmony. Start with the Brain Fork waving over the head area, then move down to the lungs, then the liver, pancreas, stomach, etc. until you have done all the Organs. During this process place the, stone- bloodstone in the center of the clients chest to stimulate blood flow, place a hematite at the feet area to ground the session, place an aurauralite at the right side of the head of the healing table, and the left side of the table place a pyrite, these stone deal with blocking out or transmuting negative energy. Make sure that the healing table is setting over or under a sacred healing space to improve the healing process.

Then consult the Ultimate Protocol Guide at the end of this volume for specific stones and tuning forks used on aliments, conditions and dis-ease.

LEVEL 4

A Brief History of Intuitive Emotional Release

Intuitive Emotional Release (I.E.R.) is hands-on and the use of tuning forks approach to, emotional release, that opens "doorways" that have been closed by deeply held fear, anger and trauma. I.E.R. is a journey that takes us back to remembrance and direct experience of the emotional trauma that caused the blockage, pain, etc.

Intuitive Emotional Release is about removing barriers from our cellular body and receiving our light and remembering who we really are. We are already enlightened; it's only about remembering and embodying this into our cells. There are doorways throughout the body that when opened allow us to access our own light. Once we can access our own light, healing takes place within. I.E.R.™ works very much with the heart. There are many barriers in our hearts and while there are barriers here one cannot receive one's own light or give out in a true form.

In I.E.R.™ there are certain areas that relate to certain emotions. For example, there are childhood tapes that keep us in the same sabotaged loop. There are anger, sexual, and fear areas all keeping us from remembrance of our divine selves. This work returns us to our natural state as free will beings. Each one of us has a gift to bring. While sometimes we are prisoners of our emotions, such as fear and shame, we may be stopping ourselves from doing what we need to be doing in this world.

Intuitive Emotional Release ™ is used at times in conjunction with vibrational yoga therapy, crystaline reiki, intuitive cranial release, spiritual healing, shamanic healing, and other progressive healing methods to create a deep profound healing for the client.

Intuitive Emotional Release is a spiritual, hands on method of facilitating emotional release and growth, either on your own or within the therapist/client setting.

"Emotional Release" means to release painful feelings that have become trapped within us, or suppressed, instead of having been cleared when they first occurred. Traditional psychotherapy has assumed that the origins of suppressed feelings is in childhood, and it has been found that progress can be made based on this assumption; there is usually a childhood component to our major issues. Transpersonal psychology, however, has broadened the scope and effectiveness of feelings work by suggesting that the roots of our most difficult feelings and circumstances are in past existences, and in our karma.

However, while Intuitive Emotional Release Therapy agrees with the possibility of this broader view, it is important that I.E.R.T. is a present-centered therapy. We work with present issues, and our feelings as they are now. The key understanding here is that while feelings may have originated in the past, they become projected onto present circumstances; as we clear feelings now, we are clearing the residue of the past. And, often we find in deeper Intuitive Emotional Release Therapy work that past memories either of childhood or beyond spontaneously come up into awareness if needed. On the other hand, it is common to find that issues become cleared with no past recall coming up or being needed to complete clearing a present issue.

The capacity for feeling and managing emotions is of utmost importance. Emotions are our connection to life; without them we are stale, hollow, and cut off from true fulfillment, but when they get out of control, we experience distress and discouragement.

Self-blocking occurs on the emotional level, not the mental or intellectual level. The emotional level is where we are most unconscious. People who have achieved self-acceptance and emotional mastery have developed the capacity for feeling deeply, without resistance, whatever is happening in their inner life. Most of us do not do this but block feelings from entering consciousness, resulting in emotional imbalance and confusion.

By using I.E.R.™ we can move forward on our journey to wholeness. We can release the unnecessary emotions that are holding us back from being our core self.

All I.E.R. is done in side a gate of grace or sacred healing space, and uses tuning forks to balance the chakras prior to the sessions emotional release process is begun.

Have a direct physical experience of what your life would feel like if there were no limitations! Repressed emotional energy locked in the body can block your ability to experience all the joy and potential that life has to offer. This can lead to stress and ultimately to disease. Releasing this blocked energy from the body and the subconscious mind can help you to achieve freedom from worry, pain and suffering, and lead you to joy, happiness and emotional freedom. Charles Lightwalker takes you to the Core of your emotional issues and helps you to identify and release what, where, and how along the way you took on a negative belief system or energetic pattern that is keeping you blocked or stuck, and release it. Have you ever had a physical/energetic experience of yourself at your highest potential? Charles Lightwalker can help you experience this. During the session you will have the opportunity to take a look at your life, identify what's not working for you, feel the energy of the life you would like to live, and release any patterns or blocks that may be keeping you from attracting your highest and greatest potential. You will be working one-on-one with Metis Shaman, healer and teacher, Charles Lightwalker, developer of the Intuitive Emotional Release ™.

Charles has researched, practiced and facilitated transformational healing systems for over 25 years. Charles is skillfully able to help you identify and release your deepest core issues and have a heartfelt experience of unconditional love and self-acceptance. This is a powerful gift to give to yourself, whether you are a corporate executive, mother, therapist or teenager. Anyone is any walk of life can benefit from the increased energy and expanded awareness that accompanies the release of this stagnant emotional energy from the body and subconscious mind. Private Sessions

Intuitive Emotional Release works with the body and the subconscious mind simultaneously to help you identify what, where and how along the way you took on a negative pattern, belief system or emotion that you are still holding onto from the past, and release it.

A Private Session is 1-1/2 to 2 hours in length. Charles has developed an integrated system, which opens gateways into the emotional body, and allows repressed emotional energy that has been held locked in the body and the subconscious mind to come to the surface to be released. During the session, Charles will balance the body using tuning forks, apply crystals or stones to the body, and Charles will ask a series of questions designed to query the subconscious mind, and stimulate the memory of what you are holding onto that is keeping you blocked or stuck in unwanted patterns, behaviors, negative thoughts and emotions. Based upon your answers, he asks the next question. Through the skillful asking of the questions, he is able to take you to the core of your emotional issues. He simultaneously goes to the appropriate area of the body and releases the blocked energy. At the end of the session Charles will use Crystaline Reiki to enhance the ongoing healing process that is accruing.

Intuitive Emotional Release is an effective treatment for releasing emotional memories held deeply within the body causing unhealthy spiritual, psychological or physical conditions. The result is to access and resolve emotional blocks as efficiently as possible, which calls for working with the body as well as the subconscious mind.
A private session of this work is profound and life-changing! Clearing the blocks which have kept you from experiencing the full range of your emotions results in increased energy and a deep personal empowerment.

This work is truly unique. One session is generally enough to clear the life template and identify the core issues which have kept you from experiencing emotional freedom in your career, relationships, and self-esteem. Subsequent sessions can take you even deeper into your transformational process.

By the end of the session, you are able to achieve a level of clarity of body, mind and spirit that goes beyond what you have ever experienced. From this place, Charles helps you to make a connection with your higher self, and with what you would truly want to do in this lifetime, if there were no limitations. This experience of unconditional confidence, and expanded sense of awareness and positive sense of Self, helps you to go beyond self-limiting patterns and behaviors, and frees you up to experience your life from a positive perspective. The cathartic emotional release that occurs brings about new energy, new insight and a freedom from negative, unhealthy issues from our past.

By the end of session, you are in a new place of inner peace, clarity, and connection with Self and Source, which represents a new level of your personal growth and spiritual evolution.

Reclaim your personal power with Intuitive Emotional Release Therapy! As children, we have a tendency to take on negative patterns, emotions and belief systems. These negative and unwanted patterns and perceptions are held as blocked energy in the physical body and negative patterns in the subconscious mind.
As and adult, you are able to clear the tendency to manifest and take on these patterns!

As blocks clear, the natural free flowing of energy through the body is restored. Along with it comes the natural self-confidence, creativity and ability to love and be loved that we originally had as children, before social conditioning and trauma contributed to cause the erosion of the child spirit.

Intuitive Emotional Release gives you the opportunity to quickly and effectively identify, examine and release your negative patterns, emotions and belief systems, and positively reinforce the ones that contribute to your success and happiness.

How IER Works

How May You Benefit from Intuitive Emotional Release?

- Experience less pain and hurt. Feel more joy and love in your life.
- Deal with difficult situations much more effectively and without comprising integrity.
- Become more aware of what you really want and expect out of relationships - family, friends, or spouse.
- Stop behaving in destructive ways.
- Deal with addictions most effectively by getting to the source of the cause of the addiction.
- Improve all aspects of your life - relationships, relaxation, sleeping, health, and much more.
- Make decisions easier when you can feel the difference between the choices. Life will begin to become less confusing.
- Dealing with Traumatic memories.
- Find meaning in life and start to see how you fit into this world and your importance in being here.

What Happens During an Intuitive Emotional Release Session?

Your first Intuitive Emotional Release session will be a little different from all the rest.
In the first session, I will give a 10-minute introduction and preparation regarding how to approach the releasing process.

I will go over some of the different ways that will help you to start to be able to begin to focus on the feelings inside of you, and the breathing process used to release these emotions that have remained stuck with in you.

All of my release work is done in a safe and gentle manner, which makes it easy for even a beginner to use this process. It starts with what you are feeling right at that moment.

The feelings could be something you are aware of or something that you had no idea you were feeling because some feelings are subconscious.

Once the session begins and you start to feel, what happens next can vary quite a bit, but it will continue to progress towards more awareness of the feelings you hold inside. It will enable you to begin to release held-in feelings and be able to feel other emotions of which you might have not been aware.

At a certain point when I feel you are ready, I will help you to start "re-programming" yourself. This is the cathartic, healing aspect of releasing work where you can get some of your deepest emotional needs met.

LEVEL 5

A Brief History of Reiki

Reiki was a system that was devised in ancient Atlantis. It was created by a high priest at the Temple of Healing, who is now known as the Ascended Master St Germain. This priest took himself away from the central temples at Atlantis, and journeyed to the far mountains of Atlantis creating his own tribe, or clan, of Atlanteans called the Inspirers. The Inspirers disconnected themselves from the mainland Atlantean dwellers. They sought to find a technique and way to equalize the spiritual development of all Atlanteans, in order to abolish and banish race differences which were judged by the psychical and spiritual progression of the Atlantean race.

Many of the Atlanteans who were considered spiritually and psychically backwards were used as slaves by the priests and priestesses and the Royal families of the Atlantean Island. St Germain in that lifetime was given a number of symbols which could be projected directly into the energy system of an individual, and which would raise their vibration to a sufficient level where they would transcend their present spiritual handicap and be equals amongst the Atlanteans. He was given twenty-two symbols, a Master number. When Atlantis was destroyed St Germain journeyed with several of his fellow brothers to ancient Tibet. They tried in this place to continue this practice of raising spiritual Consciousness. In order to see how this practice would ensue they gave three symbols to a number of individuals who were in close proximity to the Atlantean landing. Many of them used the symbols and the spiritual evolution that they brought well.

Others however used this power in a dark negative and baneful way. They perverted and contorted the symbols, transforming and changing them. St Germain and the Inspirers decided at this time not to give the full twenty-two symbols to any individuals, in order to keep the full power that they thought would corrupt these individuals minds from their grasp. The Reiki system as it is practiced today is an incomplete system. It is a system which comprises of many symbols, some which are directly drawn from the Akashic records and have been given to mankind by St Germain, but some which have been invented, created and draw upon a different type of energy. The Challenge As he took the podium one Sunday in the late 1800's, Dr Usui noticed a half dozen students in the front pew. Usually students sat at the back. One of the students immediately raised a hand. He stated that the six were co graduate in two months. but before leaving they wanted to settle an issue. First they wanted to know if Dr Usui had absolute faith in the Bible as it reads'? "Yes." Then did he believe that „Jesus could heal by laying on hands'? again Dr Usui said he did believe. The student said that he and the others also wanted to believe and would Dr Usui please give them one demonstration. Would he please heal the blind or cure the lame or just simply walk on water? Dr Usui said that although he believed these things had been done. he himself had not learned to do them. The spokesman said, "Thank you very much. We can only say that your belief in the Bible is a blind faith. and we do not want to have a blind faith." Dr Usui's response was that he could not demonstrate at that time but would someday like to prove it. He said he would find how to do it. then come back to show them. With that he resigned, on the spot. The next day he made plans to study the Bible in a Christian country.

The Search Dr Usui chose America. He entered a university, possibly University of Chicago, but no one is certain. He found that the Bible teachings were not significantly different from what he had studied in Japan. No one he met there knew how Jesus healed. However, while at the university, he studied other philosophies, and he found in Buddhism a passage saying Buddha healed by laying-on-of-hands. So for the remainder of his seven years in the United States, he concentrated on Buddhism, hoping to find a formula for the healing arts. He didn't. He left there to study in a Buddhist country - Japan. He returned to his own city of Kyoto. Kyoto had the most people and the biggest monasteries in Japan. He decided to visit all the monasteries starting with the largest, the Shin. At the Shin, Usui asked a monk if the Buddhist Sutras gave accounts of Buddha healing. "Yes." He asked if the 5hin monks had mastered the art of healing the body. He was told, "We monks do not have time for the physical in reaching the spiritual growth. Spiritual healing is first." Usui walked away into the jungle to visit other temples. Their stories were the same. None of the monastery monks could heal. His last stop was at the Zen temple. Here he heard again that the monks were very, very busy and had little time for the body healing - but they were sure that someday, during meditation, they would receive that great light and then they would know how to heal. Dr Usui decided to stay on and study all their secrets. He spent the next three years studying the Sutras but without success. He then got permission to stay on at the Zen temple to do independent research. Dr Usui learned Chinese, because the Japanese Sutras were translated from Chinese. He then mastered Sanskrit, because Buddha was a Hindu. While working on Sanskrit he found a healing formula. There was no mistaking what it was. but the 2,500 year old formula had to be interpreted and tested. He told himself. "I cannot guarantee myself whether I will live through it, but if I don't try the test, years of study will be wasted." He talked about his plan with the head Zen monk. The monk said Usui was a courageous man, and he could perform the test at the monastery. Usui said he would rather do it on Mount Koriyama. a mountain known as an excellent place for meditation.

The Meditation Dr Usui told the monk. "I will test myself for twenty-one days. If I do not some back on the night of the twenty-first day. on the twenty-second morning. send out a search party to find my body. I will be dead." Before departing he told the monks, "I shall go through this meditation without food - only water." He climbed the mountain. On the mountain he found an old pine near the stream. He piled up twenty-one rocks and watered them. (I don't know why).

He sat with his back to the tree with the rocks before him. He threw one rock away, then began his first meditation. He expected a phenomenon of some sort but had no idea what it might be or when. He read scripture, chanted, meditated. and drank water. He had no food with him. Days and nights came and went. The pile of stones dwindled. There was no phenomenon. Nothing. On the twenty-first day, he work before dawn and threw away the last stone. The morning black was near absolute - no moon. no stars. Dr Usui meditated, knowing it was the last time. He opened his eyes expecting to see nothing, but there, on the horizon, he glimpsed a flicker of light. like a candle! He instinctively knew this was the phenomenon he had hoped for - and feared. Dr Usui braced himself. "It is happening and I am not going to even shut my eyes. I shall open them as wide as I can and witness what happens to the light." The light moved towards him. It seemed to be accelerating as it approached. Usui became frightened, his courage faltered. "Oh, the light!

Now I have a chance to avoid the light, to dodge! What shall I do!? If the light strikes me. I might burn!" But he began to brace himself. "This is best. I am not going to run away! I'm going to face it! Come! If this must be. hit me!! I am ready!" :and with that. he relaxed and, with eyes wide open, he saw the light strike in the centre of his forehead. "I made contact." he said as he fell backward from the force. When he came to, he thought that he had died because at first he couldn't see and he felt nothing. The light was gone. He heard roosters in the distance and knew it would soon be dawn. Dr Usui sat, dazed. Then, off to his right, colored bubbles seemed to rise from the earth. Millions and millions of bubbles in rainbow colors danced before him. then moved to his left. Usui counted seven colors. "This is phenomena! I was blessed today!" A great white light came from his right. Golden symbols appeared, one after another. They radiated out in front of him, like on a movie screen, as if to say, "Remember! Remember!" He didn't read them so much with his eyes as with his mind. He studied and studied. then said, "Yes!" He recalled all he had learned in Sanskrit as the symbols moved in front of him as if they were saying, "This is it. this is it. Remember, remember." After the phenomena had passed. lie said "I must close my eyes. and for the last meditation please give me a vision." He closed his eyes and saw the golden symbols in front of him. The Miracles It was over. "'Now. I can open my eyes."

As he regained awareness of his body. he was surprised to find no pain or hunger. "I feel my body is good. I'm going to stand up." He stood. "':My legs and feet are strong. I fast for twenty-one days. and still I feel I can walk back to Kyoto." his body felt well fed. "Well, this is a miracle- I'm not hungry. And I feel very light." He dusted himself off, picked up his cane and straw hat, then took the first steps of his twenty-five mile trek to Kyoto. The Zen monks were expecting him by sundown. Near the foot of the mountain, Dr Usui stubbed a big toe on a rock.

The blow lifted the toenail. Blood spurted out. It hurt. The pain thumped with his heartbeat. He sat down and held the toe in his hands. The pain subsided. The bleeding stopped. "Is it okay?"

He continued to hold it till there was no more pain. Then he looked at the toe, he was amazed and delighted to see the nail back in its normal position. There was no indication of injury except dried blood. "This is a second miracle!" A short distance later. he came upon a traditional mat and ashtray, which means in Japan there is an eating place near by and that all are welcome. He approached an old, unshaven man who was starting a fire in a hibachi. "Good morning old man." "Good morning, my dear monk, you are early." "Yes, I know. but may I have some leftover rice and some tea, and that piece of nori you just made? And I would like to have some salted cabbage and also some dried fish, if you have some." (This is a typical Japanese breakfast.) But the old gentleman was wise. He had served many monks after their extended meditations on this famous mountain. He knew the appearance of a seven day beard; he knew this monk had been without food for a much longer time. "I cannot let you have this rice and hot soup and all those other things, because you are going to have a huge indigestion. I have no medicine and cannot help you. Kyoto is far away. You will have to wait until I make a soft gruel." "Thank you. You are very kind, but I think I shall try it." Dr Usui was feeling weak as he moved to a table to wait for the food. The old man thought, "Well, if he wants to do it his way, fine. I am not responsible." Soon, the man's fifteen Year old granddaughter brought a tray with lots of food.

She was crying and had a towel wrapped under her chin, tied in rabbit ears on top of her head.

"My dear young girl, why do you cry." The child sobbed. "Oh, my dear monk, three days and three nights I have a toothache so bad that I cannot stop my tears, and I cannot eat the whole time. The dentist is too far away, so I just suffer and cry." Dr Usui s heart opened to the child. He stood and put a hand on her swollen cheek. The girl began to blink her eyes. Dr Usui soon had both hands on her face. She suddenly cried out, "'My dear monk, You have just made magic! The toothache is gone!" Usui could hardly believe it. He hadn't really known what to expect from his impulsive action. "Is it really'? Are you telling me the truth?" It was true. she quickly removed the rabbit ears and was radiantly happy. Usui said. "Yes. now I believe you are well. – the beaming child thanked him. then she ran off to her grandfather. "Look grandfather. I took off my rabbit ears! The toothache is gone? He is not an ordinary monk. he makes magic!!" The grandfather. wiping his hands on his apron. walked over to Dr Usui. "My dear monk. you did us a great service. We are grateful. We do not have money but for our gratitude. there is no charge for the food. This is all we can offer." Dr Usui said, "Thank you! I will accept your gratitude. Thank you, very much. Now for my food." With that he turned to his food and eagerly shoveled it with chopsticks. He ate happily. The people watched and hoped this magic monk wouldn't suffer any kind of indigestion. Later. Dr Usui reflected on these miracles. the third and fourth.

Placing his hands on the child had again healed almost instantly, and he had suffered no ill effects from breaking a twenty-one day fast with a huge meal. "'Now. I am ready for my hike to the Zen temple. I shall be there by sundown according to schedule." · And so he was. The doctor was met at the temple gate by a young page boy. Dr Usui asked, "How is our dear monk?" "Oh, he's suffering from arthritis and back ache. He is in bed near the chapel stove." Before going to visit the monk, Usui went to his own room to bathe and put on clean clothes. He was then taken to the monk. "My dear monk, I am back. :My meditation was 'a success." The ailing monk was excited by this news and wanted the details. Dr Usui said. "Yes, of course, and while I talk. may

I place my hands on your silk covers?" It was late at night when the doctor shared the last happy detail. He was about to leave when the old monk spoke up, "And by the way, my pain is all gone. I can sleep now. I don't need the stove, and my body feels wonderful - you say this is called Reiki?" (In English. Reiki means Universal Life Energy.)

The Reiki Experiment Dr Usui slept in a bed for the first time in three weeks. Next morning, after breakfast, Dr Usui presented a question to all the temple monks. "What shall I do to experiment with this Reiki?" After much discussion it was decided that the best way to experiment was to go into one of the very big slums in Kyoto. The slums were playgrounds for most every kind of injury and disease including leprosy. They chose the largest slum. Dr Usui walked into the slum as a monk vegetable peddler - dressed as a monk with two baskets of vegetables hanging from a pole. The beggars assembled quickly. Usui told them. "Please, I would be one of you. I would like to live here." in turn, he was told, "If you want to stay here, we have a chief. We shall call him." Shortly the chief beggar made his appearance. "I understand that you want to live here and become one of us." Usui answered yes. "In that case. give us vegetables. And there is no need to wear new clothes here. we will give you initiation clothes. they undressed Dr Usui and found his money belt. The chief beggar said he had known the belt was there and that it would also have to be forfeited. Dr Usui was then allowed to dress in his beggar initiation costume - dirty. smelly rags. The chief asked what Dr Usui was going to do in the slum. "I would like you to provide me with food and a cottage by myself. Then you can send me your sick and I will heal them." The chief found that to be a very good trade. "We have all kinds of diseases. even tuberculosis and leprosy. You are not afraid to touch them'? The doctor said as a healer he was not afraid of disease and promised to work sunup to sundown, so he would want meals delivered to the cottage. Agreed? The next day many appeared at his door.

Based on his own theory. the doctor categorized the sick. He believed disease was an effect resulting from some inner cause. He felt that in the younger patients the cause should be shallow and more easily treated. And this is the way it worked out. The older slum dwellers required more Reiki treatments and recovery sometimes took months. The young healed quickly. Usui sent healed patients to the Zen temple where they received a new name and a job in the city. He told them to become honest citizens, to forget the slums. One evening, after seven long, hard years of Reiki healing, he was out walking through the slums when he spied a vaguely familiar face. "Who are you?" "Oh, you should remember. I was one of the first healed. The temple monks gave me a new name and found me a job. But now I am back. Begging is easier than hustling by myself." This was the greatest shock of the doctor's life. He threw himself to the ground and cried, cried like a heart broken child. Most of his former patients returned to the slums. Dr Usui now realized that after all the years of searching for a healing formula and these years in the slums. He had become preoccupied with the physical side of life; he had forgotten the spiritual. "Oh. what did I do? I did not save a soul. 5o the physical is number two and the spiritual is number one. All the churches were right. I was wrong. No beggars. no more beggars, no more beggars. It is my fault they come back. I did not teach them gratitude. They are here because they are greedy, greedy people. Want, want, want- nothing in return. If I had taught them the spiritual side first, then healed the body, it would have been effective. no more beggars. No more healing." Dr Usui turned his back on the slums and walked away.

I would suggest reading the book Atlantean Reiki, and Crystal Reiki to enhance your Reiki practice.

Dr. Chujiro Hayashi

It was at one of these lectures, in about 1925, that Dr Usui is said to have met 45 year old Dr Chujiro Hayashi, a retired Naval Commander. Dr Usui pointed out to Hayashi that he was too young to retire, and invited him to join him in his crusade. Dr Hayashi accompanied him on his tour of Japan for many years, continuing his system of healing after Dr Usui's death around 1930. It was Dr Hayashi who passed the story of Dr Usui on to Mrs. Takata, saying that he had not changed Dr Usui's original system; although it is claimed that it was Dr Hayashi who developed the system of standard hand positions, the three degrees and their attunement processes. He opened a very successful clinic in Tokyo, where Mrs. Takata became one of his patients. In about 1941 he predicted the approach of a great war, (World War II) and realized that most of the men would be called up, including some of the 16 Reiki Masters that he had already created, so in order to preserve his development of Reiki, he passed his complete teachings on to two women, his wife Chie and Hawayo Takata, whom he named as his successor. As a Naval reserve officer, he had already been drafted, but as a healer he refused to take life. On May 10, 1941, in front of several of his students, he psychically stopped his own heart, and chose his own death. Born in 1900 in Hanamaulu, on the island of Kauai, Hawaii, her parents, Mr. & Mrs. Otogoro Kawamura, were poor immigrants from Japan, working as pineapple cutters. They had great hopes for their daughter and her future, naming her Hawayo after the territory of Hawaii. But she was never physically strong, being too small for plantation work. Instead she took several part time jobs whilst still at school, and on leaving became a servant at the plantation owner's house. During the next twenty-four years she managed to work her way up to the position of housekeeper and bookkeeper. In 1917 she married the plantation accountant Saichi, whom she describes as a guiding light in her life, until his early death in October 1930, from a heart attack. The strain of trying to bring up two young daughters on her own took its toll upon her health. She developed asthma, nervous exhaustion, and gall-bladder disease. Following the death of her sister in 1935, she traveled to Tokyo to take the news to her parents, who had retired there. It was whilst she was there that she entered the Maeda Medical Hospital in Akasaka, where she was diagnosed with a tumor, gallstones and appendicitis. Her poor respiratory condition, of course, made the possibility of an operation very dangerous.

However, she rested there for several weeks, and was eventually scheduled for surgery. The night before her operation she heard a voice telling her that it would not be necessary. She again heard the same voice, whilst lying on the operating table, being prepared for the anesthetic. On reporting this to the surgeon, and enquiring if there were any other treatment that she could take, he told her that his sister had attended Dr Hayashi's clinic, and had herself been trained there.

The very next day she took Mrs. Takata to the clinic, where she remained for four months, receiving regular treatments from the teams of healers working there. Mrs. Takata asked to be trained in Reiki also, but was at first refused, because she was considered a foreigner, and it was not in Dr Hayashi's plans for the practice of Reiki to leave Japan. But Mrs. Takata persisted, and finally, with the intervention of the surgeon who had originally told her of Reiki, in Spring 1936 she received her first Reiki I attunement. She went on to take her Reiki II, remaining at the clinic and becoming part of the team of healers there, returning at last to her home in Hawaii in 1937.

In 1938 Dr Hayashi followed her to Hawaii, where he lectured with her, assisted in the setting up of her clinic, and gave her a Reiki III initiation. On February 22, 1938 her announced her as a Master, and in 1941 made her his successor. Despite his insistence that she did not give any training away without charge, she passed free attunements to her friends and relatives. But she found that instead of using this knowledge to heal others, they continued to bring all their patients to her, not having any faith in their own abilities. It was at about this time that her sisters asked her for free attunements also, and were most upset when she refused. She suggested that if they could not afford the fees, they could perhaps pay in installments, and this was agreed upon as a satisfactory compromise. Her sister was later reported by Mrs. Takata to have said that it was the cheapest investment that she made, better than buying a car! Mrs. Takata later noted that of all the twenty four people that she gave free attunements to, not one of them had went on to attain good health themselves, or were successful in business. Contrary to popular thought, Mrs. Takata was not rigid in her thinking, but grew and expanded upon her own personal experiences.

However, she did acknowledge that an exchange of energy in some form was necessary for the healing to be effective. It seems that we value most that which we have made an effort to obtain.

Mrs. Takata eventually traveled to the United States, and then on to Canada, spreading the knowledge of Reiki as she went. Where she found people who were seriously ill, she trained a member of their family to give them healing. She taught Reiki in many different ways, varying the hand positions and even the symbols that she taught, responding always to the needs of her students. During the last ten years of her life she trained twenty-two Reiki Masters, both men and women, until her eventual death on December 11, 1980. Since then Reiki has spread all around the world, to all continents, with an estimated 6,000 Masters, and some 600,000 practitioners.

Defining Reiki

Essentially, "Reiki" is a term used to refer to a system of healing and self-development created by Mikao Usui in Japan in the early part of the 20th Century.

While commonly referred to simply as "Reiki" or "Reiki Therapy ", the original system of healing and self-development is more formally called "Usui Reiki Ryoho" - that is: "Usui Reiki Healing Method" or "Usui Reiki Treatment"

Reiki is also known variously as: Usui Shiki Ryoho (Usui-style Healing Method [/Treatment]) Usui Do (the 'Do' refers to a spiritual or philosophical 'path', or 'way') Usui Teate ('Teate' - means 'treatment', 'therapy' or 'hand-healing') and Usui Reiho (Spiritual Method) [some people seem to think Reiho is a ....contraction of 'Reiki Ryoho']

Simply stated, the Reiki Therapy can be said to be a synergistic combination of 'spiritual healing' and 'energy healing' techniques.

While the system has been influenced by spiritual and therapeutic discipline, practice and ideals found within Shinto, Buddhism (and possibly Taoism), Reiki itself has no specific religious affiliation.

Reiki - a generic term of latter years, however, the word 'Reiki' has, it seems, achieved generic status.

Much as the word: 'Hoover' is used to refer to the vacuum cleaner in general - no matter what particular form or style or manufacturer - so, the word: 'Reiki' has, at various times, been applied to all manner of forms of 'energetic' healing.

It has been used to refer to the hands-on practices of certain South American Shamans, to forms of western Spiritualist Healing, to high-level Chinese Chi Gung healing practices (and has even been cited by some as the means used by Jesus, Buddha, and many other religious figures to enact healing miracles).

Admittedly, many people - having undergone Reiki training - have taken the essential phenomenon that is at the very core of Reiki Therapy and successfully integrated it into various spiritual, cultural and esoteric belief-systems and practices. This has resulted in the manifestation of numerous viable and effective new 'styles' of Reiki, or what at least may be referred to as ' 'Reiki-influenced', therapeutic modalities and systems of personal development.

Reiki - Energetic Radiance

However, technically (and certainly in the context of these Reiki Pages), the term "Reiki" is properly solely used to indicate the therapeutic and self-development system created by Mikao Usui.

More specifically, the name "Reiki" identifies the wonderful therapeutic energy radiance, or phenomenon, which lies at the heart of this natural healing system.

The "Rei" part of the name is often translated as "Universal*", and in essence, it refers to something Spiritual or Sacred, and can mean "Soul".

"Ki", is often translated simply as "Life-Force Energy", yet also implies 'Spiritedness' or 'Feelings'.
Thus, depending on one's perspective, Reiki can be understood as:" Universal* Life-Force Energy", "Spiritually-influenced Life-Force Energy", or even as "Charismatic Healing Radiance".

* 'Universal' in this sense, originally being a contraction of: 'the Universal' - an alternative (and intentionally less religious) term for 'the Divine', 'Numinous' , 'God''.

Reiki - a gentle therapy

Reiki is a gentle, yet profound, non-invasive therapy, which can facilitate stress-reduction and relaxation, support effective immune-system function, enhance the body's self-healing mechanisms, and replenish and nurture vitality.

Rather than acting solely on a physical level, Reiki is holistic in its effect - eliciting a healing response across the entire spectrum of ones being - physical, mental, emotional and spiritual.

It can prove beneficial in the resolving of physical disorders, nervous conditions and emotional issues, and help nurture a greater sense of balance, well-being, and wholeness in ones life.

Reiki can be effectively used in combination with other therapies - both allopathic and 'alternative' - and has been shown to effectively stimulate the relaxation response.

The Reiki Principles

Central to the Reiki system of wellness and self-development is a set of 5 guiding Principles or Precepts - referred to in Japanese as the: gokai.

These principles - affirmed morning and night, and kept in ones thoughts throughout ones daily activities - are intended to assist in transforming ones attitude to life, and bring the soul/self into balance, enabling one to respond with compassion in all situations.

Reiki after Hawayo Takata

Gradually, after Hawayo Takata's death, several of the Reiki Masters she had certified began to modify elements of the way in which they practiced Reiki, and also, the way they taught it to their own students.

These modifications were essentially a matter of personal preference, and the results of experimentation with independently evolved techniques, and practices 'adopted' from other therapeutic disciplines.

Over the following years, the number of Reiki practitioners grew exponentially, with Reiki spreading to the U.K., Europe and many other places around the globe.
Hawayo Takata's teacher, Chujiro Hayashi, had committed suicide in 1940, and after that, it seems, all contact with other Reiki practitioners in Japan was lost.

The general concensus amongst Usui Shiki Ryoho Reiki practitioners was that, partly as a result of W.W.II, the practice of Reiki had actually died out in Japan, and that, Master Takata had been the only remaining Reiki Master alive.

However, in 1985, a journalist named Mieko Mitsui who had studied one of the modified forms of Reiki (known as 'the Radiance Technique', or 'Real Reiki') while living in New York, went back to Japan to see what she could discover about Reiki's origins.

She started teaching Reiki there and in the process could be said to have been responsible for single-handedly sparking a 'Reiki Revival' in Japan.
In addition to promoting the style of 'western' Reiki, Mieko reported that, contrary to previous belief, Reiki had never actually died out in Japan. Since it's introduction into the United States Reiki has undergone changes in its adaptation to and connection to other forms of energy healing.

Crystalline Reiki

What is crystaline reiki? "Rei" meaning universal and "ki" or energy, is an energetic system of healing which utilizes attunements to enable the student to effectively channel the universal life force. Crystaline is an increased frequency of reiki energy. Attunements means that through the energetic manipulations of the person's aura, a Master may unlock or otherwise enable a person's ability to channel Reiki (universal energy) through them. This Crystaline Reiki energy does not require any of the practitioner's personal energy, nor can it ever be used in any way other than in a beneficial manner or effect, in other words, Crystaline Reiki never exhausts person. It is similar to a radio and its antenna-that is, the energy comes through the antenna and passes through with no effect on the instrument. In fact, residual beneficial energy, because it is healing energy, will heal the practitioner as well as the person receiving the Crystaline Reiki.

The energy comes down through the crown chakra and out the palms of the Crystaline Reiki practitioner. Only a Crystaline Reiki Master, because they have received the Master attunements, can bestow attunements, and the ability to pass attunements. Attunements are termed this because they essentially "attune" a person to the frequency and vibration of the Crystaline Reiki or universal life force, thus enabling the person to attune to the Crystaline Reiki and pass it through them.

Crystaline Reiki can be used for present (hands-on) or distant (absent) healing, and it heals on the physical mental, and emotional as well as the spiritual levels.

There are four levels of Crystaline Reiki: I, II, Master, and Master Teacher. Basically, the beginning Crystaline Reiki I practitioner is taught to heal (hands-on) and to do self healing.

Crystaline Reiki II involves sacred symbols, which are used to enhance healing (hands-on) and also to accomplish distant healing.

The Master/Teacher level is for those who may be interested in teaching and passing attunements. Crystaline Reiki at all levels will enhance your spiritual growth.

There are at least three and possibly four main areas or organizations or schools of Reiki. In broad terms there is traditional Usui, non-traditional, Crystaline, ancient forms and others. Reiki is part of the ancient knowledge of the Tibetan Buddhists. Reiki may have been taught in Lemuria and later, Atlantis. It's origins are really hazy, but probably those who left us the Vedas and texts in India may have been the earliest recorded knowledge of this ancient healing art. It is said that this energy is similar to that which was exhibited in healings by Jesus and other sainted personages. Our belief is that Crystaline Reiki is ability and a gift, which lies within each of us. It is only waiting to be unlocked and shared. So if you wish to be of services to others, learn a valuable healing method, and generally grow spiritually learn Crystaline Reiki now.

Glossary of Reiki Terms

A

Adama StarFire Reiki is another form of Reiki energy that is channeling to the Earth from the stars.
Ai-Reiki The state of being in harmony with Reiki
Angelic RayKey (Reiki) is a healing discipline for the 21st Century. The focus is on healing and uplifting all areas of living: body, mind, and spirit.
Anshin Ritsumei (also: Dai Anjin) - a state in which ones mind is totally at peace - not bothered by anything - and in which one perceives one's life's purpose.
Ascension Reiki is about opening up to this great outpouring of Love.

B

Brahma Satya Reiki has evolved out through a spiritual descent of Shiva-Shakti in the form of Brahma Satya
Byosen Reikan-ho Also simply called `Byosen'. A Reiki technique for sensing energetic fluctuations

C

Chakra Kassei Kokyo-ho Chakra-activating breathing method
Celtic Reiki: a form of Reiki discover by Martyn Pentecost of Croydon U.K. and employs symbols derived from the Celtic ogham (the ancient alphabet used by the Druids).
Choku Rei Name of the first of the four Usui Reiki symbols. Commonly called the 'Power' symbol in Takata-lineage Reiki (Usui Shiki Ryoho). In Japanese lineages the symbol is commonly called the 'Focus' symbol' [some relate it to the earth element]. Takata-Sensei translated Choku Rei as 'put the [spiritual] power here', yet it can also translate as something akin to: `in the presence of the Spirit(s)'.
Crystal Reiki: a form of Reiki by Geoffery Keytes of the United Kingdom
Crystaline Reiki: A form of reiki founded during meditation by shamanic reiki master Charles Lightwalker.

D

Dai Ko Myo Name of the last of the four Usui Reiki symbol. Commonly called the 'Master' symbol in Takata-lineage Reiki (Usui Shiki Ryoho). The ` symbol' is actually the words Dai, Ko, & Myo written in kanji, and name literally means: 'Great Shining Light' - signifying 'Enlightened Nature' or 'the Radiant Light of Wisdom' - the Radiance of a Deity (Buddha, Bodhisattva, 'Vidyaraja', etc) - the manifest expression of the Light of Wisdom: the means by which illumination "dawns on us."
Denju 'Initiation' - the 'Western' style Reiki attunement process used by Takata-Sensei
Divine Light Reiki is a new system based on the Japanese system Jôrei, or Johrei, that was developed in the early 20th century by Mokichi Okada, founder of the Church of World Messianity.
Dragon Reiki By Victor Glanckopf
Dolphin Reiki: a form of Reiki by Shanti Johnson

E

Eguchi te-no-hira Ryoji A hand/palm healing modality developed by Toshihiro Eguchi (- a friend and student of Usui Sensei), said to incorporate elements of Usui-do Enkaku Chiryo-Ho 'Distant Healing Method'
Excalibur reiki In this Reiki system you will be attuned to the energy of Excalibur, the Sword of Truth. You will learn how to tap into the archetypal energies of Merlin and the Lady of the Light to heal and manifest.

F

G

Gakkai A 'Learning Society' - such as the Usui Reiki Ryoho
Gakkai Gassho A ritual gesture formed by placing the hands together in a prayer-like position in front of the mouth - the fingertips at a level just below the nose.
'Gassho' implies recognition of the oneness of all beings. This gesture is also used to show reverence to Buddhas, Bodhisattvas, Patriarchs & Teachers Gassho Kokyu-Ho
'**Gassho Breathing Method**' - the practice of 'breathing' through the hands while in the Gassho position
Gassho Meiso Gassho Meditation
Gendai Reiki Ho 'Modern Reiki Method' - modern form of Japanese Reiki created by Hiroshi Doi - combines some traditional Usui teachings & techniques with teachings & techniques from other energy-healing arts Gendoku-Ho Detox technique - one hand is placed at seika tanden, the other on the lower back at approximately the same level
Gold Reiki There isn't a lot of information available on Gold Reiki. However, it is considered to be very powerful Reiki of the Gold Ray. Transmutes fear and darkness into light and joy! Gold Light is the strongest light of transformation in the physical universe! The Gold Ray is a very purifying Ray.
Gokai The Five Reiki Principles / Precepts Gokai Sansho Recitation of the Five Reiki Principles / Precepts (sansho here refers to 'three times')
GrandMaster Reiki- The highest level of Reiki, where one can create their own symbols.
Gyosei Poetry penned by the Meiji Emperor, about 125 of which are recited / sung at meetings of the Usui Reiki Ryoho Gakkai. [These poems are in a style known as waka]
Gyoshi-Ho 'Gazing Method' - technique of healing with the eyes

H

Hado Kokyu-Ho Breathing technique, said to raise ones vibrational levels Hado Meiso Ho Hado-breath meditation
Hanshin Chiryo-Ho 'Half-body Treatment Method'
Hanshin Koketsu-Ho **'Half-body Blood-purifying Method'**
Hara 'Belly' - the extended area between the top of the pubic bone and the base of the sternum
Hatsurei-Ho Generate [/Invoke] (Hatsu), Spirit (Rei), Method (Ho) - a set of primarily Ki-jutsu techniques which Usui Sensei is said to have taught as an aid to self-development
Heso Chiryo-Ho Acupressure-type energy-balancing technique applied to the navel with middle finger
Hibiki 'Reverberation' - sensation in the hands, the nature of which can indicate the presence and status of a dis-ease
Hikari no Kokyu-Ho 'Breath of Light' Method - a variant of Joshin Kokyo-Ho
Hikkei A handbook or manual
Hon Sha Ze Sho Nen Name of the third of the four Usui Reiki symbol. Commonly called the 'distant' symbol in Takata-lineage Reiki (Usui Shiki Ryoho). This ' symbol' is actually the words: Hon, Sha, Ze, Sho, &Nen, written in kanji (albeit in a stylised form). While some people have sought to translate the phrase 'Hon Sha Ze Sho Nen' as: "no past, no present, no future", this mantra phrase actually translates as: 'Mindfulness is the essence of Being' (or alternatively - 'Correct Thought is the root for everything'). It does not represent an energy, but a state of mind - a connectedness to all things.

I

Imara Reiki requires that you have already reached the level of Reiki Master to receive full benefit from this course. Imara is incredibly powerful, yet it does not need symbols. Imara is recognized as Level V on the Reiki energy scale that some people use. Imara Reiki uses a new and easy attunement process. Barton Wendel first channeled Imara.
In-Yo Equivalent of the Chinese Yin-Yang

J

Jaki Kiri Joka Ho Technique for 'energetic cleansing' of inanimate objects. NOT to be used on living things: people, plants or animals [This technique seems to be derived from a more involved practice called the 'Ki Barai'] Jikiden Reiki 'Original Teaching' or 'Directly Taught' Reiki - Japanese Reiki as taught by Chiyoko Yamaguchi - a student of Chujiro Hayashi Joshin Kokyo-Ho Cleansing Breathing technique used to stimulate, strengthen and purify the flow of Reiki - a component of
Hatsurei-Ho Jumon A Mantra or Sacred Invocation

K

Kaicho A president / chairman - title of the Leader of The Usui Reiki Ryoho Gakkai Kanji Chinese characters used for writing Japanese
Kanboku A term used to indicate the Reiki symbols by Yuji Onuki - a student of Toshihiro Eguchi [see also shirushi]
Kantoku Illuminating visionary mystical state - brought about by practice of strict ascetic mystical disciplines including fasting, isolation, meditation & the use of incantation and mudra-like techniques

Karmic Reiki is an exciting style of Reiki style created by Martyn Pentecost, which although based on Usui Reiki techniques, is used in a slightly different manner in order to deal with the various issues that arise from negative karmic events.
Karuna Reiki, Karuna is a Sanskrit word and is used in Hinduism and Buddhism. Developed by William Rand
Karuna Ki is an advanced form of Reiki developed by Vincent Amador.
Kenyoku-Ho 'Dry Brushing Method' - essentially an aura-cleansing technique - a component of Hatsurei-Ho
Ketsueki Kokan-Ho The Reiki 'Finishing' or 'Smoothing' technique
Ki-jutsu 'Energetic Arts' - Collective term for Japanese disciplines concerned with the development, strengthening and refinement of 'Ki'
Ki Ko Japanese name for the Chinese Art of Chi Gung (Qi Gong)
Kiriku Pronounced: k'rik - the 'spiritual emblem' of Amida Butsu, and probable origin of the second of the four Usui Reiki symbols - Sei Heiki Koketsu-Ho 'Blood-purifying Method' Koki-Ho 'Exhalation (Koki) Method' - technique of healing with the breath Kokoro Heart, Spirit, Will or Mind Kokyo-Ho Breathing Techniques for Development, Strengthening and Purification of Ki **Koshin-do Mawashi** The 'Reiki Circle' method. [also called Reiki Mawashi]
Kotodama 'Word-Spirit' - Shinto practice involving the intonation of individual syllables and vowel-sounds
Kouki With Zenki, one of the two inner levels comprising Okuden, the second level of Reiki training.
Kundalini Reiki Founder of Kundalini Reiki Ole Gabrielsen
Kurama Yama Horse-saddle (Kurama) Mountain (Yama) - the Sacred Mountain where Usui-Sensei is believed to have first experienced Reiki [though some have suggested Mount Koya as the original site]

L

Laxmi Reiki Master Lakshmi or Laxmi is the Hindu goddess of Wealth, fortune and luck.
Lavender Flame of Quan Yin is a fraction of the Violet Flame of Transmutation.
Light Dream reiki was channeled in 2003 by Alla Sharkia. Light Dream Reiki works well for those suffering from insomnia. There are no symbols in this method and this is highest frequency based on the power of the Violet Ray of St. Germain
LUNAR LIGHT Reiki EMPOWERMENT From the Founder of Kundalini Reiki: Ole Gabrielsen

M

Makoto No Kokyu A Hara Defining Exercise contained in the two inner levels of Okuden (Zenki & Kouki), being one of many different meditations and energy exercises taught at these levels. This is a very powerful meditation and has been practised in Japan since the 8th century, but it is much older - probably about 2000 years old.
Medicine Buddha Reiki is a well-known healing practice, and many believe that it originates from the Buddhist tradition.

N

Nade-Te Chiryo-Ho Stimulating the flow of ki in the body by stroking with the hand
Nentatsu-Ho Form of 'thought-transmission' via the hands

O

Okuden Level II in some versions of the Reiki Grading system
Oshite Chiryo-Ho `Pressing Hand' - actually, an acupressure-type technique applied with the fingertips

P

Q

R

Raku Kei Reiki Master The words Rei-Ki originate from the words Raku-Kei. It is thought to have been a forerunner of Reiki and incorporates the Fire element of breathing used to increase the energy of Reiki. Raku-Kei is the ancient science of Self-development and Self-improvement
Ra-Sheeba Reiki Founders: Merilyn Bretherick and Peter Johansen of Victoria Australia describe Ra-Sheeba as follows. People want to know what "Ra-Sheeba" Energy is, where does it come from and what does it do. As these energies are in the early stages here is what as been found so far. Ra-Sheeba is a very powerful section of the available Universal Healing Energy.
Rei To Bow - as in: Kamiza ni Rei [bow to the Altar], Otagai ni Rei [bow to fellow students], Sensei (Gata) ni Rei [bow to ones teacher(s)], Shinzen ni Rei [bow to a shrine.], Ritsu (or Tachi) Rei [standing bow], Za Rei [kneeling bow]. By bowing, you are expressing respect, courtesy, and gratitude to your art, your sensei, dojo (training establishment), other students, and yourself [This `rei' is not written in the same kanji as the `rei' in `Reiki']
Reiho Etiquette; a method of bowing Reiho `Spiritual Method' -as in: Usui Reiho: Usui Spiritual Method Some people claim that `Reiho' is a contraction of: `Reiki Ryoho' (Reiki Healing Method) This `Reiho' is not written in the same kanji as the `Reiho' meaning Etiquette] Reiji `Indication of the Spirit' - Spiritual guidance in the placing of your hands to give treatment
Reiju Spiritual (Rei) Gift (Ju) - term for the original form of Reiki Attunement-Empowerment Reiki The term commonly used to indicate the therapeutic and self-development system created by Mikao Usui, and more specifically, the wonderful therapeutic energy radiance, or phenomenon, which lies at the heart of this natural healing system. (However, the word `Reiki' has, it seems, achieved generic status, being used to refer to numerous hands-on healing practices of unrelated origin.) Reiki can translate as: `Spiritual Energy', `Spiritual Feeling', and in some instances can be used as a term for an Ancestral Spirit.
Reikika A Reiki Practitioner `Reiki Ryoho No Shion' `Kind Teacher's Reiki Method of Healing' - the title of a Reiki manual said to be given to all members of the Usui Reiki Ryoho Gakkai Reiki Un-do A method of Reiki treatment received through spontaneous movement - albeit intentionally initiated
Renzoku A `Reiki marathon' Ryoho `Healing Method; Medical Treatment' -as in:Usui Reiki
Ryoho: Usui Reiki Healing Method

S

Sacred Flames Reiki (SFR) is a powerful system compiled by Allison Dahlhaus from different resources (in the physical and spiritual realms) to share with all those drawn to it. SFR is a set of guided visualizations and meditations designed to help the body, mind, and spirit heal themselves, and/or to maintain good balance within the systems of the body, both physically and energetically.

Saibo Kassei Ka A cell-activating technique

Seichim, (pronounced say-keem), is an Egyptian word meaning power. It was discovered in 1984 by an American Reiki Master, Patrick Zeigler, much in the same mystical way as Dr. Usui received Reiki.

Seiheki Chiryo-Ho A variant form of Nentatsu-Ho Sei Heiki The second of the four Usui Reiki symbols: commonly called the 'mental/emotional' symbol in Takata-lineage Reiki (Usui Shiki Ryoho). In Japanese lineages the symbol is commonly called the 'Harmony' symbol' [some relate it to the water element].Depending on the kanji used to write 'Sei Heiki', the name can mean 'emotional calmness' or 'spiritual composure'

Seiza Traditional Japanese kneeling posture, sitting back on (or between) the heels Sekizui Joka Ibuki-Ho Spinal Cord (Sekizui) Purification (Joka) Breath (Ibuki) Method (Ho) - a technique of 'insufflation' or blowing of energy-breath to release negativity from the spine Shiki 'Style' - as in Usui Shiki Ryoho: Usui Style Healing Method

Shinpiden Level III (Master Level) in some versions of the Reiki Grading system Shirushi 'Symbol' Shoden Level III in some versions of the Reiki Grading system

Shu Chu Reiki Reiki Treatment given to a single individual by a group

Spirit Reiki is a system of spirit growth and healing that is available to Usui Reiki Masters. This system uses two Usui Reiki symbols as well as four additional symbols that were given to Linda Jean Horton.

Sufi Reiki takes healing to the next level, empowering the individual to move beyond an awakening and toward the self-realisation.

T

Tibetan Reiki is a system of energy healing that helps to bring our energies into balance and harmony.

Tanden Chiryo-Ho A body detoxification technique Te-Ate 'Hand-Treatment' - generic term for Japanese hands-on healing modalities

U

Uchite Chiryo-Ho A Shiatsu-like patting or palpating technique

Usui A term used by many Japanese shamanic practitioners to describe 'power spots' - places where the 'veil' between this world and the World of the Spirit is thin. (Usui = Thin). However, in this instance, 'usui' -although having the same sound - is written in different kanji than the surname

Usui / Usui Do 'Usui's Way'. Term used to refer to Usui-sensei's original system of Spiritual Development.

Usui Reiki Ryoho 'Usui Reiki Healing Method.' Term used to refer to Reiki as it evolved in Japan. Said to be closer to Usui-Sensei's original format. Utilises Reiju rather than the symbol-centred attunements familiar in 'western' style Reiki.

Usui Reiki Ryoho Gakkai (Usui Reiki Healing Method Learning Society). While some say the society was founded by Usui-Sensei himself in 1922, it is generally accepted that the Gakkai was actually founded by Rear Admiral Juusaburo Gyuda (Ushida) and other students around 1926/7.

Usui Shiki Ryoho 'Usui Style Healing Method'. 'Western' Reiki as taught by Takata-Sensei -a system divided into 3 levels, using attunements involving the four Reiki symbols.

Usui Teate 'Usui Hand Treatment'. Term used by some of Usui-Sensei's surviving students to refer to his Healing Method.

V

Violet Flame Reiki, a form of Reiki using the violet flame as part of the healing process.

W

Waka `Japanese Song' - short poems with lines containing fixed numbers of syllables. [The familiar Zen haikyu are a form of waka]

White Dove Reiki™ Although there are many forms of Reiki, White Dove Reiki™ enables the Reiki Practitioner to have assistance in the Healing and Attunement process.

X

Y

Yagyu Ryu Usui Sensei is believed to have achieved the high ranking of `Menkyo Kaiden' in **Yagyu Ryu,** a Bujutsu (Martial Arts) School focusing on the arts of Kenjutsu (Swordfighting) & **Ju-jutsu** (Un-armed Combat) - founded by Yagyu Muneyoshi Tajima no Kami (1527-1606).

Z

Zenki With Kouki, one of the two inner levels comprising Okuden, the second level of Reiki training.

Zenshin Koketsu-Ho Full-body Treatment Method

End Materials

IDENTIFICATION WORKSHEET

Date :	Stone:	Stone History:

Color	Streak	Fracture/Cleavage	Hardness	Luster	Crystal Form
	Taste	Magnetic	Effervescence	Birefringence	Birefringence

Date :		Stone:		Stone History:	
Color	Streak	Fracture/Cleavage	Hardness	Luster	Crystal Form
	Taste	Magnetic	Effervescence	Birefringence	Birefringence

IDENTIFICATION WORKSHEET

Date :		Stone:		Stone History:	
Color	Streak	Fracture/Cleavage	Hardness	Luster	Crystal Form
	Taste	Magnetic	Effervescence	Birefringence	Birefringence

Date :	Stone:	Stone History:			
Color	Streak	Fracture/Cleavage	Hardness	Luster	Crystal Form
	Taste	Magnetic	Effervescence	Birefringence	Birefringence

IDENTIFICATION WORKSHEET

Date :	Stone:	Stone History:			
Color	Streak	Fracture/Cleavage	Hardness	Luster	Crystal Form
	Taste	Magnetic	Effervescence	Birefringence	Birefringence

Date :	Stone:	Stone History:			
Color	Streak	Fracture/Cleavage	Hardness	Luster	Crystal Form

	Taste	Magnetic	Effervescence	Birefringence	Birefringence

DISCLAIMER

This information describes complementary health techniques that may help to facilitate the healing of one's physical, emotional, mental, and spiritual bodies.

We do not diagnose or treat medical or psychological conditions or diseases.

It is not the author's intent to encourage people into purchasing educational material or products to diagnose or treat medical conditions.

As always in the event of any of the symptoms described here in you should seek the advice of a professional health practitioner.

The information provided in this manual is for educational purposes only.

LEGAL INFORMATION

Depending on where you live, there are many state and federal laws that you will have to deal with. Unless you are a licensed health care practitioner, such as a Medical Doctor, Chiropractor, or Acupuncturists, you will not be permitted to do or say the following with clients:

Do not "diagnose" any illness or complaint. Remember you can instead say that you are detecting or observing a blockage in the flow of energy.

Do not say you can "cure" someone's disease or problem. Healers cannot claim they "cure" anything. You can instead say that you will help the client heal themselves.

If during the course of your healing you notice blockages in their energy flow, you cannot make a "referral" to a medical doctor to your client. Making a referral implies that you have made a diagnosis. You can suggest that the client seek out other healthcare practitioners, for other opinions or assistance in their healing journey.

Never, ever, tell someone your that your healing practice is a viable replacement for the medical treatment that they are taking. Using Tuning forks and Crystals and Gemstones is a "complementary " practice.

And <u>never</u> tell your clients or anyone to stop taking their medicine. You can encourage them to seek advice fro their healthcare provider, but nothing more.

This legal information is provided as a reminder to check with the local laws in your state or area, before practicing holistic health care methods of treatment.

Ultimate Protocol Guide Levels 1-5

The following information is given as a general protocol in using gemstones, tuning forks, IER, and Reiki in the healing process.

A

Abdominal Pains
Tuning Forks: Stomach fork, 3rd Chakra fork, Adrenal fork, and Nerve fork, place stem on effected area, for 20 seconds 3 times with each fork.
Gems & Crystals: Citrine, Golden Topaz, Green-Yellow Tourmaline, Tiger's Eye, Heliodor, Rutilated Quartz, Amber, Sunstone, Malachite, Peridot and Emerald.
IER: after using the tuning forks and Gemstones, have the client breathe into the abdominal area, press lightly on the out breath, repeat 2 times.
Reiki: Apply the Reiki with the hands over the stones for 15 minutes

Acne
Tuning Forks: 1st Chakra, 2nd Chakra, 3rd Chakra, 4th, and circulation fork, blood fork, wave over the acne area for 1 minute each fork.
Gems & Crystals: Green-Yellow Tourmaline, Tiger's Eye, Amber, Moonstone, Cornelian
IER: after using the tuning forks and Gemstones, have the client breathe into the affected area, press lightly on the out breath, repeat 3 times.
Reiki: Apply the Reiki with the hands over the stones for 15 minutes

Aches and Pains
Tuning Forks: See pain relief booklet more details, use of Nerve fork Om fork and others.
Gems & Crystals: Golden Topaz, Green-Yellow Tourmaline, Tiger's Eye, Heliodor, Rutilated Quartz, Amber
IER: after using the tuning forks and Gemstones, have the client breathe into the affected area, press lightly on the out breath, repeat 4 times.
Reiki: Apply the Reiki with the hands over the stones for 15 minutes

Addictions
Tuning Forks: Use all the forks, balance the chakras retune the organs and use the DNA fork by waving over the entire body. Seal in with Creation fork.
Gems & Crystals: Sugilite, Ametrine, Clear Quartz Crystal, Amethyst, Howlite, Moonstone, Lavender Quartz, Rutilated Quartz, Diamond and White Topaz.
IER: after using the tuning forks and Gemstones, have the client breathe into the abdominal area, press lightly on the out breath, repeat 3 times.
Reiki: Apply the Reiki with the hands over the stones for 15 minutes

Adenoid Problems
Tuning Forks: Use 5th Chakra fork, and 7th chakra fork
Gems & Crystals: Amethyst, Howlite, Moonstone, Amber
IER: after using the tuning forks and Gemstones, have the client breathe into the abdominal area, press lightly on the out breath, repeat 2 times.
Reiki: Apply the Reiki with the hands over the stones for 15 minutes

Adrenal
Tuning Forks: Use Adrenal fork with balancing the chakras first (also recommended retune the organs)
Gems & Crystals: Amber, Sunstone, Malachite, Peridot and Emerald, place the stones just below the breastbone left side of body for 20 minutes
IER: after using the tuning forks and Gemstones, have the client breathe into the adrenal area, press lightly on the out breath, repeat 3 times.
Reiki: Apply the Reiki with the hands over the stones for 15 minutes

AIDS
Tuning Forks: Balance the Chakras and organs use adrenal fork with Sekheim, DNA fork and creation fork
Gems & Crystals: Morganite, Kunzite, Green Aventurine, Ruby, Hiddenite, Grossular Garnet, Green Jade, place the stones on the heart area leave for 30 minutes.
IER: after using the tuning forks and Gemstones, have the client breathe into the abdominal area, press lightly on the out breath, repeat 6 times.
Reiki: Apply the Reiki with the hands over the stones for 15 minutes

Allergies
Tuning Forks: Use 3, 4th, 5th, and 6 the chakra forks, wave over body 3 times 20 seconds each
Gems & Crystals: Azurite, Sugilite, Amethyst, Celestite, Tanzanite, Blue Tourmaline, Sapphire, Lavender Quartz, Purple Fluorite, Charoite, Sodalite, Iolite, place these stones on the forehead leave for 15 minutes.
IER: after using the tuning forks and Gemstones, have the client breathe into the sinus area, press lightly on the out breath, repeat 2 times.
Reiki: Apply the Reiki with the hands over the stones for 15 minutes

Alzheimer's
Tuning Forks: Balance Chakras, and use creation fork and DNA fork over entire body for 15 minutes using the two forks together
Gems & Crystals: Howlite, Moonstone, Lavender Quartz, Rutilated Quartz, Diamond, White Topaz, place on chest area leave for 12 minutes
IER: after using the tuning forks and Gemstones, have the client breathe into the chest area, press lightly on the out breath, repeat 2 times.
Reiki: Apply the Reiki with the hands over the stones for 15 minutes

Anemi
Tuning Forks: Balance Chakras, the use Mineral forks (Iron, Molybdenum, Copper) over center of body 8 inches above the body for 10 minutes each fork
Gems & Crystals: Pyrite, Sugilite, Ametrine, place on upper half of body for 15 minutes.
IER: After using the tuning forks and Gemstones, have the client breathe into the chest area, press lightly on the out breath, repeat 3 times.
Reiki: Apply the Reiki with the hands over the stones for 15 minutes

Anger
Tuning Forks: Balance chakra then, Use Mineral fork (Manganese) figure eight over entire body, then seal in with Creation fork.
Gems & Crystals: Tiger's Eye, Heliodor, Rutilated Quartz, Amber, Sunstone, Malachite, Peridot, Emerald, place the stones on the stomach area leave for 15 minutes.

IER: after using the tuning forks and Gemstones, have the client breathe into the abdominal area, press lightly on the out breath, repeat 6 times.
Reiki: Apply the Reiki with the hands over the stones for 15 minutes

Angina
Tuning Forks: Balance chakras, then use Gallbladder fork, Oxygen fork, and Circulation fork for 10 minutes then seal in with Creation fork.
Gems & Crystals: Rutilated Quartz, Amber, Sunstone, Malachite, Peridot, Emerald, place the stones on the stomach area leave for 15 minutes.
IER: after using the tuning forks and Gemstones, have the client breathe into the abdominal area, press lightly on the out breath, repeat 2 times.
Reiki: Apply the Reiki with the hands over the stones for 15 minutes

Ankle Problems
Tuning Forks: (See Pain relief booklet) Use Nerve fork on area, circulation fork and Oxygen fork for 5 minutes by waving over painful area.
Gems & Crystals: Bloodstone, place on the ankle leave for 20 minutes
IER: after using the tuning forks and Gemstones, have the client breathe into the ankle area, then visualize releasing the on the out breath, repeat 2 times.
Reiki: Apply the Reiki with the hands over the stones for 15 minutes

Anxiety
Tuning Forks: Use Om fork, balance chakras, use liver fork (Om and liver 5 minutes each waved over entire body)
Gems & Crystals: Citrine, Golden Topaz, a place over the stomach area for 15 minutes.
IER: after using the tuning forks and Gemstones, have the client breathe into the abdominal area, press lightly on the out breath, repeat 2 times.

Appendicitis
Tuning Forks: Use 1st, 2nd, and 3rd chakra forks, place stem on area for 5 minute each fork
Gems & Crystals: Amber, Sunstone, Golden Beryl, Aragonite, Orange Calcite, lay stones on the area of the pain.
IER: after using the tuning forks and Gemstones, have the client breathe into the abdominal area, press lightly on the out breath, repeat 1 time.
Reiki: Apply the Reiki with the hands over the stones for 15 minutes

Arms Problems
Tuning Forks: Use Oxygen fork, nerve fork, and circulation fork, seal with Creation fork, slide forks along the arm area for 4 minutes each fork
Gems & Crystals: Amazonite, Lapis Lazuli, Larimar, Sodalite, Iolite, Kyanite lay on the arm for 15 minutes a day.
IER: after using the tuning forks and Gemstones, have the client breathe into the arm area, press lightly on the out breath, repeat 3 times.
Reiki: Apply the Reiki with the hands over the stones for 15 minutes a day.

Arteries
Tuning Fork: Use Blood fork, Circulation fork, Oxygen fork, 4th chakra fork and Creation fork, place fork on heart area for 6 minutes each fork
Gems & Crystals: Nephrite, Kunzite, Prehnite, Chrysoprase, Rhodonite, Moldavite, Prasiolite, lay on area near heart.
IER: after using the tuning forks and Gemstones, have the client breathe into the chest/heart area, press lightly on the out breath, repeat 2 times.

Reiki: Apply the Reiki with the hands over the stones for 15 minutes

Arthritis
Tuning Forks: Use Circulation fork, oxygen fork, Nerve fork, DNA fork and Creation fork use on areas for 5 minutes each fork
Gems & Crystals: Bloodstone, Kunzite, Green Aventurine, Ruby, lay on affected areas for 20 minutes each day
IER: after using the tuning forks and Gemstones, have the client breathe into the affected area, press lightly on the out breath, repeat 2 times.
Reiki: Apply the Reiki with the hands over the stones for 15 minutes

Asthma
Tuning Forks: Use Lung fork, Circulation fork, Oxygen fork and Creation fork wave over area for 10 minutes each fork
Gems & Crystals: Rose Quartz, Pink Tourmaline, Rubellite, Rhodochrosite, Emerald, Green Tourmaline, Malachite, Morganite, lay over the lung area for 20 minutes 3 time a day.
IER: after using the tuning forks and Gemstones, have the client breathe into the chest/lung area, press lightly on the out breath, repeat 2 times.
Reiki: Apply the Reiki with the hands over the stones for 15 minutes

Athlete's Foot
Tuning Forks: Use Circulation fork, 2nd, 3rd, 4th, 6th Chakra forks and DNA fork, use each fork for 3 minutes each waving over entire foot, seal with Creation fork.
Gems & Crystals: Cornelian, Garnet, Ruby, Cuprite, Black Tourmaline, Smoky Quartz, Onyx, Agate, Black Obsidian, Hematite, lay on the affected foot (feet) for 10 minutes 3 times a day.
IER: after using the tuning forks and Gemstones, have the client breathe into the feet, press lightly on the out breath, repeat 2 times.
Reiki: Apply the Reiki with the hands over the stones for 15 minutes

B

Back Problems
Tuning Forks: (See DNA fork, use for 5 minutes each fork waving over entire back area except Bladder fork place on bladder area for 5 minutes, then seal in with Creation fork.
Gems & Crystals: Cornelian, Garnet, Ruby, Cuprite, Black Tourmaline, Smoky Quartz, Onyx, Agate, lay on the back for 20 minutes a day.
IER: after using the tuning forks and Gemstones, have the client breathe into the back area, press lightly on the out breath, repeat 3 times.
Reiki: Apply the Reiki with the hands over the stones for 15 minutes

Bedwetting
Tuning Forks: Balance Chakras, then use Bladder fork, Colon fork, each for 5 minutes each, and seal in with Creation fork
Gems & Crystals: Amber, Moonstone, Cornelian, Citrine, Golden Topaz, Golden Beryl, Aragonite, Orange Calcite, Selenite, lay the stones on bladder area 10 minutes a day.
Bedwetting (cont.)
IER: after using the tuning forks and Gemstones, have the client breathe into the bladder area, press lightly on the out breath, repeat 3 times.
Reiki: Apply the Reiki with the hands over the stones for 15 minutes

Bladder Problems

Tuning Forks: Use Bladder fork, Circulation fork, Oxygen fork, DNA fork, 5 minutes each then seal with Creation fork
Gems & Crystals: Amber, Moonstone, Cornelian, Citrine, Golden Topaz, Golden Beryl, Aragonite, Orange Calcite, Selenite, lay the stones on bladder area 10 minutes a day.
IER: after using the tuning forks and Gemstones, have the client breathe into the bladder area, press lightly on the out breath, repeat 2 times.
Reiki: Apply the Reiki with the hands over the stones for 15 minutes

Bleeding
Tuning Forks: Use Blood fork, Iron fork (from Mineral Set), 10 minutes each fork then seal with Creation fork
Gems & Crystals: Bloodstone, Agate, Grossular Garnet, Green Jade, lay near area of bleeding.
IER: Do Not Use IER on Bleeding problems.
Reiki: Apply the Reiki with the hands over the stones for 15 minutes

Blood Problems (*Pain Relief Booklet*)
Tuning Forks: Balance Chakras, then use Blood fork, Circulation fork, Oxygen fork, work on Lymphatic System (see Booklet) seal in with Creation fork.
Gems & Crystals: Bloodstone, Agate, Grossular Garnet, Green Jade, Quartz Crystal, lay on the heart area for 20 minutes a day.
IER: after using the tuning forks and Gemstones, have the client breathe into the chest/heart area, press lightly on the out breath, repeat 2 times.
Reiki: Apply the Reiki with the hands over the stones for 15 minutes

Blood Pressure (High)
Tuning Forks: Use Blood fork (see chart in Pain Relief Booklet), 4th Chakra fork, Circulation fork, Oxygen fork, Selenium fork (Mineral Set) use each fork for 5 minutes each then seal with Creation fork.
Gems & Crystals: Bloodstone, Green Jade, Ruby, Hiddenite, lay on upper part of chest near heart area 15 minutes a day.
IER: after using the tuning forks and Gemstones, have the client breathe into the chest area, press lightly on the out breath, repeat 4 times.
Reiki: Apply the Reiki with the hands over the stones for 15 minutes

Blood Pressure (Low)
Tuning Forks: Repeat above process but use the Iron fork (Mineral Set) instead of Selenium fork
Gems & Crystals: Bloodstone, Kunzite, Green Aventurine, Malachite, Morganite, lay on the lower part of the chest near heart area for 10 minutes per day.
IER: after using the tuning forks and Gemstones, have the client breathe into the chest area, press lightly on the out breath, repeat 2 times.
Reiki: Apply the Reiki with the hands over the stones for 15 minutes

Bone Problems
Tuning Forks: Balance the Chakras, use Bone fork, Iron Fork, Muscle fork, and DNA fork then seal in with Creation fork.
Gems & Crystals: Hematite, Pink Tourmaline, Rubellite, Rhodochrosite, lay on affected areas for 15 minutes per day.
IER: after using the tuning forks and Gemstones, have the client breathe into the bone area, press lightly on the out breath, repeat 2 times.
Reiki: Apply the Reiki with the hands over the stones for 15 minutes

Bowel Problems
Tuning Forks: Use Colon fork, Bladder fork, 1st and 2nd Chakra forks, wave over area then use Creation fork.
Gems & Crystals: Black Tourmaline, Smoky Quartz, Onyx, Agate, Black Obsidian, Hematite, Fire Agate, Ametrine, lay on the bowel area for 20 minutes a day.
IER: after using the tuning forks and Gemstones, have the client breathe into the bladder area, press lightly on the out breath, repeat 2 times.
Reiki: Apply the Reiki with the hands over the stones for 15 minutes

Brain Problems
Tuning Forks: Use Brain fork after balancing the Chakras, then use the Third Eye fork and Om fork, place stem of forks on each side of the head on the indentation and on the third eye area. (use the Opening Psychic Pathways Booklet) End with Creation fork.
Gems & Crystals: Ametrine, Clear Quartz Crystal, Amethyst, Howlite, Moonstone, Lavender Quartz, lay stones on the forehead for 10 minutes three times per day.
IER: after using the tuning forks and Gemstones, have the client breathe into the brain area, press lightly on the forehead out breath, repeat 2 times.
Reiki: Apply the Reiki with the hands over the stones for 15 minutes

Breast Problems
Tuning Forks: Use 4th chakras fork, Lungs fork, Oxygen fork, wave over area for 5 minutes each fork, then use Creation fork
Gems & Crystals: Rose Quartz, Emerald, Green Tourmaline, lay on breast area for 20 minutes a day.
IER: after using the tuning forks and Gemstones, have the client breathe into the breast area, press lightly on the forehead out breath, repeat 2 times.
Reiki: Apply the Reiki with the hands over the stones for 15 minutes

Bronchitis
Tuning Forks: Use Oxygen fork, Lung fork, 4th Chakra fork, 5th Chakra fork, Wave fork over the area for 5 minutes each fork, then use the Creation fork.
Gems & Crystals: Apophyllite, Aquamarine, Blue Lace Agate, Blue Topaz, Blue Tourmaline, Celestite, lay on the chest area for 20 minutes a day.
IER: after using the tuning forks and Gemstones, have the client breathe into the chest area, press lightly on the forehead out breath, repeat 3 times.
Reiki: Apply the Reiki with the hands over the stones for 15 minutes

Burns
Tuning Forks: Use Zinc fork (Mineral Set), DNA fork, Oxygen fork, Circulation fork, use each fork for 5 minutes, wave over area, then use Creation fork.
Gems & Crystals: Bloodstone, Charoite, Sodalite, lay gently on the burn area for 5 minutes 3 times per day
IER: Do Not use IER on Burns.
Reiki: Apply the Reiki with the hands over the stones for 15 minutes

Bursitis
Tuning Forks: Balance Chakras, Muscle fork, Oxygen fork, use 3 times per day 5 minutes per fork, then use Creation fork.
Gems & Crystals: Bloodstone, Lavender Quartz, Purple Fluorite, Amazonite, Lapis Lazuli, lay on affected area for 10 minutes per day.

IER: after using the tuning forks and Gemstones, have the client breathe into the bursitis area, press lightly on the forehead out breath, repeat 2 times.
Reiki: Apply the Reiki with the hands over the stones for 15 minutes

C

Cancer
Tuning Forks: Use Oxygen fork, Shekinah fork, Creation fork, use them in combination with each other alternating them every 3 minutes for 20 minutes.
Gems & Crystals: Amber, Sunstone, Malachite, Cornelian, Garnet, Ruby, Cuprite, lay on the body between heart and stomach in circle pattern for 20 minutes a day.
IER: after using the tuning forks and Gemstones, have the client breathe into the affected area, press lightly on the out breath, repeat 2 times.
Reiki: Apply the Reiki with the hands over the stones for 15 minutes

Cataracts
Tuning Forks: Use Lightly waving over the eyes, the creation fork, 6th Chakra fork, Third eye fork, and DNA fork, daily for 10 minutes.
Gems & Crystals: Amethyst, Celestite, Tanzanite, Blue Tourmaline, Sapphire, Lavender Quartz, lay on eyes for 20 minutes 3 times per day.
IER: after using the tuning forks and Gemstones, have the client breathe into the eyes area, press lightly on the forehead out breath, repeat 2 times.
Reiki: Apply the Reiki with the hands over the stones for 15 minutes

Cellulite Reduction
Tuning Forks: Use the Fat Cell fork with Muscle fork then massage area, then use Creation fork
Gems & Crystals: Bloodstone, Yellow Tourmaline, Tiger's Eye, Heliodor, lay on area for 20 minutes a day.
IER: after using the tuning forks and Gemstones, have the client breathe into the affected area, press lightly on the out breath, repeat 2 times.
Reiki: Apply the Reiki with the hands over the stones for 15 minutes

Cervical Cancer
Tuning Forks: Balance Chakras, the use Creation fork, Shekinah fork, and Oxygen fork, wave over area for 20 minutes
Gems & Crystals: Bloodstone, Yellow Tourmaline, Tiger's Eye, Heliodor, Amber, Sunston, lay on area for 20 minutes a day.
IER: after using the tuning forks and Gemstones, have the client breathe into the affected area, press lightly on the cervical area on the out breath, repeat 2 times.
Reiki: Apply the Reiki with the hands over the stones for 15 minutes

Cholesterol Problems
Tuning Forks: Balance Chakras, do Lymphatic System Protocols, and seal with Creation fork
Gems & Crystals: No specific stones recommended
IER: after using the tuning forks and Gemstones, have the client breathe into the abdomen area, press lightly on the stomach area on the out breath, repeat 2 times.
Reiki: Apply the Reiki with the hands over the stones for 15 minutes

Chronic Fatigue

Tuning Forks: Balance Chakras, Endocrine and Lymphatic Systems Protocols, Mineral Set, Nerve fork and then use Creation fork to seal session
Gems & Crystals: Aurauralite, wear a pendent.
IER: after using the tuning forks and Aurauralite, have the client breathe into the abdomen area, press lightly on the stomach area on the out breath, repeat 2 times.
Reiki: Apply the Reiki with the hands over the stones for 15 minutes

Circulation Problems
Tuning Forks: Use Circulation fork, Oxygen fork, Blood fork, 4th Chakra fork, and then use Creation fork
Gems & Crystals: Pink Tourmaline, Rubellite, Rhodochrosite, Emerald, Green Tourmaline, Malachite, Morganite, lay stones on chest area on heart for 15 minutes 3 times a day.
IER: after using the tuning forks and Gemstones, have the client breathe into the chest area, press lightly on the chest area on the out breath, repeat 2 times.
Reiki: Apply the Reiki with the hands over the stones for 15 minutes

Cirrhosis
Tuning Forks: Balance Chakras, Liver fork, Blood fork, use Stem Cell Protocols, and seal with Creation
Gems & Crystals: Citrine, Golden Topaz, Green-Yellow Tourmaline, Tiger's Eye, Heliodor, lay on the liver area of the body for 15 minutes 2 times a day.
IER: after using the tuning forks and Gemstones, have the client breathe into the chest area, press lightly on the chest area on the out breath, repeat 2 times.
Reiki: Apply the Reiki with the hands over the stones for 15 minutes

Colds and Influenza
Tuning Forks: Balance Chakra, then use Lung fork, Oxygen fork, Liver fork, Nerve fork, use each fork for 5 minutes , three times a day, then seal with Creation fork.
Gems & Crystals: Bloodstone, Green Aventurine, Ruby, Hiddenite, Grossular Garnet, Green Jade, lay stone on chest area for 15 minute 2 time a day.
IER: after using the tuning forks and Gemstones, have the client breathe into the chest area, press lightly on the chest area on the out breath, repeat 3 times.
Reiki: Apply the Reiki with the hands over the stones for 15 minutes

Colitis
Tuning Forks: Balance Chakras, then use Stomach fork, Colon fork, Liver fork, Nerve Fork (if there is pain) then use Creation fork to seal in session.
Gems & Crystals: Golden Topaz, Golden Beryl, Aragonite, Orange Calcite, Selenite, Zircon, lay stones on the lower stomach area for 15 minutes 3 times a day.
IER: after using the tuning forks and Gemstones, have the client breathe into the chest area, press lightly on the chest area on the out breath, repeat 2 times.
Reiki: Apply the Reiki with the hands over the stones for 15 minutes

Confidence, Lack of
Tuning Forks: Balance Chakras, then use Phosphorus fork, Brain fork, for 5 minutes each and then seal in with Creation.
Gems & Crystals: Ametrine, Clear Quartz Crystal, Amethyst, Howlite, Moonstone, Lavender Quartz, lay stones on the forehead for 15 minutes 3 time a day
IER: after using the tuning forks and Gemstones, have the client breathe into the forehead area, press lightly on the forehead area on the out breath, repeat 2 times.
Reiki: Apply the Reiki with the hands over the stones for 15 minutes

Congestion
Tuning Forks: Balance Chakras, Oxygen fork, Circulation fork, Lung fork, use these fork for 5 minutes each, then seal in with Creation fork
Gems & Crystals: Green Aventurine, Ruby, Hiddenite, Grossular Garnet, Green Jade, lay stones on the stomach area for 15 minutes 2 times a day.
IER: after using the tuning forks and Gemstones, have the client breathe into the chest/lung area, press lightly on the chest/lung area on the out breath, repeat 2 times.
Reiki: Apply the Reiki with the hands over the stones for 15 minutes

Constipation
Tuning Forks: Use Colon fork, Stomach fork, Liver fork, Bladder fork, Adrenal fork for 5 minutes each then seal in with Creation fork.
Gems & Crystals: Smoky Quartz, Onyx, Agate, Black Obsidian, Hematite, Fire Agate, Ametrine, Blood Stone, lay on lower back area just above buttocks for 15 minutes 3 times a day.
IER: after using the tuning forks and Gemstones, have the client breathe into the bladder area, press lightly on the bladder area on the out breath, repeat 2 times.
Reiki: Apply the Reiki with the hands over the stones for 15 minutes

Cough
Tuning Forks: Balance Chakras, then use Oxygen fork, Circulation fork, Lung fork, Liver fork, use each fork for 5 minutes then seal in with Creation fork.
Gems & Crystals: Blue Topaz, Blue Tourmaline, Celestite, Indicolite, Blue Turquoise, lay stones on the throat area for 15 minutes 2, times a day, for 7 days.
IER: after using the tuning forks and Gemstones, have the client breathe into the chest/throat area, press lightly on the chest area on the out breath, repeat 2 times
Reiki: Apply the Reiki with the hands over the stones for 15 minutes

Cramps
Tuning Forks: Balance Chakras, then use Calcium fork, Oxygen fork, Blood fork, Circulation fork, use each fork for 4 minutes then seal in with Creation fork. For *Muscles Cramps* add in the following forks, Potassium fork, Magnesium fork.
Gems & Crystals: Bloodstone, Golden Topaz, Golden Beryl, Aragonite, Orange Calcite, Selenite, Zircon, lay stones on affected area for 10 minutes, then use the tuning forks mentioned above.
IER: after using the tuning forks and Gemstones, have the client breathe into the pelvic area, press lightly on the pelvic area on the out breath, repeat 2 times.
Reiki: Apply the Reiki with the hands over the stones for 15 minutes

Crohn's Disease
Tuning Forks: Balance Chakras, then use Stomach fork, Liver fork, Colon fork, Intestines fork, Pancreas fork, Gallbladder fork, Kidney fork, use each fork for 3 minutes each, then seal with Creation fork.
Gems & Crystals: Amber, Moonstone, Cornelian, Tiger's Eye, Heliodor, Rutilated Quartz, Amber, Sunstone, lay stones on the stomach area for 15 minutes prior to using the tuning forks.
IER: after using the tuning forks and Gemstones, have the client breathe into the hip area, press lightly on the hip area on the out breath, repeat 2 times
Reiki: Apply the Reiki with the hands over the stones for 15 minutes

Cysts
Tuning Forks: Do Lymphatic Process (see Lymphatic Manual or Tuning Fork Manual)

Gems & Crystals: Bloodstone, Emerald, Citrine, Golden Topaz, lay on area for 15 minutes 5 times per day.
IER: after using the tuning forks and Gemstones, have the client breathe into the affected area, press lightly on the affected area on the out breath, repeat 2 times.
Reiki: Apply the Reiki with the hands over the stones for 15 minutes

D

Depression
Tuning Forks: Balance Chakras, then use Iron fork, Manganese fork, Oxygen fork, Brain fork, 5 minutes each for then seal with Creation fork.
Gems & Crystals: Blue Tourmaline, Sapphire, Lavender Quartz, Purple Fluorite, Charoite, lay stones on forehead for 10 minutes 4 times a day.
IER: after using the tuning forks and Gemstones, have the client breathe into the forehead area, press lightly on the forehead area on the out breath, repeat 2 times
Reiki: Apply the Reiki with the hands over the stones for 15 minutes

Diabetes
Tuning Forks: Balance Chakras, then use Potassium Fork, Zinc fork, Chromium fork, Circulation fork, Pancreas fork, use each fork for 10 minutes, 3 times per day, then seal with Creation fork
Gems & Crystals: Citrine, Golden Topaz, Green-Yellow Tourmaline, Tiger's Eye, Heliodor, Rutilated Quartz, Amber, Sunstone, lay stones on stomach area in circle for 15 minutes 3 times a day.
IER: after using the tuning forks and Gemstones, have the client breathe into the abdomen area, press lightly on the abdomen area on the out breath, repeat 2 times.
Reiki: Apply the Reiki with the hands over the stones for 15 minutes

Diarrhea
Tuning Forks: Balance Chakras, then use Stomach fork, Colon fork, Molybdenum fork, each for 5 minutes every half hour for 3 hours, then seal in each time with Creation fork
Gems & Crystals: Amber, Moonstone, Cornelian, Citrine, Golden Topaz, Golden Beryl, Aragonite, Orange Calcite, Selenite, lay out on lower back in figure 8 for 15 minutes.
IER: after using the tuning forks and Gemstones, have the client breathe into the buttocks area, press lightly on the buttocks area on the out breath, repeat 2 times.
Reiki: Apply the Reiki with the hands over the stones for 15 minutes

Digestive Problems
Tuning Forks: Balance Chakras, then use Stomach fork, Intestine fork, Pancreas fork, Colon fork, Liver fork, use each fork for 5 minutes 2 a day, then seal in with Creation fork
Gems & Crystals: Amber, Moonstone, Cornelian, Citrine, Golden Topaz, Golden Beryl, Aragonite, Orange Calcite, Selenite, lay out on lower back in figure 8 for 15 minutes.
IER: after using the tuning forks and Gemstones, have the client breathe into the abdomen area, press lightly on the abdomen area on the out breath, repeat 2 times.
Reiki: Apply the Reiki with the hands over the stones for 15 minutes

Dizziness
Tuning Forks: Balance Chakras, then use Oxygen fork, Circulation fork, use each for 4 minutes, then seal with Creation fork
Gems & Crystals: Tanzanite, Blue Tourmaline, Sapphire, Lavender Quartz, Purple Fluorite, lay stones on forehead for 12 minutes.

IER: after using the tuning forks and Gemstones, have the client breathe into the forehead area, press lightly on the forehead area on the out breath, repeat 2 times.
Reiki: Apply the Reiki with the hands over the stones for 15 minutes

E

Ear Problems
Tuning Forks: Use 3rd, 4th, 5th, 6th Chakra fork, Oxygen forks, Circulation fork, place stem of fork on lower part of head near bottom of ear, use each fork 5 minutes then seal with Creation fork
Gems & Crystals: Howlite, Moonstone, Lavender Quartz, Rutilated Quartz, Diamond, White Topaz, lay stones around the ear making a half circle for 15 minutes 2 times a day.
IER: after using the tuning forks and Gemstones, have the client breathe into the ear area, press lightly on the out area of the ear on the out breath, repeat 2 times.
Reiki: Apply the Reiki with the hands over the stones for 15 minutes

Eczema
Tuning Forks: Balance Chakras, then use, Oxygen fork, Circulation fork, DNA fork and Creation fork, use each fork for 3 minutes each twice a day.
Gems & Crystals: Bloodstone, White Topaz, Moonstone, lay stones on the skin area for 10 minutes 3 times a day.
IER: after using the tuning forks and Gemstones, have the client breathe into the forehead area, press lightly on the forehead area on the out breath, repeat 4 times
Reiki: Apply the Reiki with the hands over the stones for 15 minutes

Elbow Problems
Tuning Forks: Balance Chakras, then use Nerve fork, Oxygen fork, Circulation fork on Elbow, 4 minutes each fork, then seal with Creation fork
Gems & Crystals: Bloodstone, Ametrine, Clear Quartz, lay elbow on these stones for 15 minutes 2 time a day.
IER: after using the tuning forks and Gemstones, have the client breathe into the elbow area, press lightly on the elbow area on the out breath, repeat 2 times.
Reiki: Apply the Reiki with the hands over the stones for 15 minutes

Emphysema
Tuning Forks: Balance Chakras, then use Oxygen fork, Circulation fork, Lung fork, Liver fork, use each fork for 6 minutes each, then seal in with Creation fork
Gems & Crystals: Blue Topaz, Blue Tourmaline, Celestite, Indicolite, Blue Turquoise, Green Aventurine, Ruby, Hiddenite, Grossular Garnet, Green Jade, lay stones in a circular pattern on the chest area for 15 minutes 4 times a day.
IER: after using the tuning forks and Gemstones, have the client breathe into the chest area, press lightly on the chest/lung area on the out breath, repeat 3 times.
Reiki: Apply the Reiki with the hands over the stones for 15 minutes

Endometriosis
Tuning Forks: Balance Chakras, then use Blood fork, Nerve fork, Stomach fork, Da"Ath fork (Use method described in Endocrine Booklet) wave forks over the Ovaries area and lower back/pelvic region, then seal in with Creation fork
Gems & Crystals: Amber, Moonstone, Cornelian, Citrine, Golden Topaz, Golden Beryl, Aragonite, Orange Calcite, Selenite, Zircon, Sunstone, Black Obsidian, Hematite, Fire Agate, Ametrine, Blood Stone, Nephrite, lay the stones over the reproductive area for 20 minutes 2 times a day.

IER: after using the tuning forks and Gemstones, have the client breathe into the reproductive area, press lightly on the reproductive area on the out breath, repeat 2 times
Reiki: Apply the Reiki with the hands over the stones for 15 minutes

Epilepsy
Tuning Forks: Balance Chakras, then use Brain fork, Nerve fork, Oxygen fork, place stem on side of head temple areas for 5 minutes each then seal in with Creation fork
Gems & Crystals: Azurite, Sugilite, Amethyst, Celestite, Tanzanite, Blue Tourmaline, Sapphire, Lavender Quartz, Purple Fluorite, Charoite, lay stones in acircular pattern on a healing table then have client lay with head resting in side the circle of stones for 15 minutes.
IER: after using the tuning forks and Gemstones, have the client breathe into the forehead area, press lightly on the forehead area on the out breath, repeat 2 times.
Reiki: Apply the Reiki with the hands over the stones for 15 minutes

Eye Problems
Tuning Forks: Balance the Chakras, then use Manganese fork, Nerve fork, Circulation fork, waving fork over the eyes for 2 minutes each 3 times per day, then seal in with Creation fork
Gems & Crystals: Tanzanite, Blue Tourmaline, Sapphire, Lavender Quartz, Purple Fluorite, Charoite, Sodalite, Iolite, lay each stone on the eyes for 5 minutes each 2 times a day.
IER: after using the tuning forks and Gemstones, have the client breathe into the eye area, press lightly on the forehead area on the out breath, repeat 2 times.
Reiki: Apply the Reiki with the hands over the stones for 15 minutes

F

Fainting
Tuning Forks: Balance Chakras, then use Blood fork, Brain fork, Oxygen fork and Circulation fork, use each fork three times a day for 4 minutes each fork, then seal in with Creation fork
Gems & Crystals: Bloodstone, place on third eye area for 10 minutes.
IER: after using the tuning forks and Gemstones, have the client breathe into the forehead area, press lightly on the forehead area on the out breath, repeat 2 times.
Reiki: Apply the Reiki with the hands over the stones for 15 minutes

Fatigue
Tuning Forks: Balance Chakras, and Organs, then use Nerve fork, Phosphorus fork, Potassium fork, Calcium fork, Zinc fork, use each fork for 10 minutes each waving over entire body, then seal with Creation fork
Gems & Crystals: Lavender Quartz, Citrine, Golden Topaz, Golden Beryl, Aragonite, Agate, Black Obsidian, Hematite, lay the stones starting at the stomach with a straight line up to the throat for 10 minutes 3 times a day.
IER: after using the tuning forks and Gemstones, have the client breathe into the abdomen area, press lightly on the abdomen area on the out breath, repeat 3 times.
Reiki: Apply the Reiki with the hands over the stones for 15 minutes

Fearfulness
Tuning Forks: Balance Chakras and Organs, then use Phosphorus fork, Calcium fork, Potassium fork by waving over the entire body for 5 minutes each fork, then seal in with Creation fork
Gems & Crystals: Azurite, Aurauralite, Sugilite, Amethyst, Celestite, Tanzanite, Blue Tourmaline, Sapphire, Lavender Quartz, Purple Fluorite, Charoite, lay the stones in a figure eight pattern on the chest and stomach area for 20 minutes 3 times a day.

IER: after using the tuning forks and Gemstones, have the client breathe into the abdomen area, press lightly on the forehead area on the out breath, repeat 2 times.
Reiki: Apply the Reiki with the hands over the stones for 15 minutes

Feet Problems
Tuning Forks: Balance Chakras and Organs, then use Nerve fork, Oxygen fork, Circulation fork waving over the feet for 5 minutes each fork, then seal with Creation fork
Gems & Crystals: Bloodstone, Aurauralite, Sugilite, Amethyst, rest the feet on the stones for 20 minutes 3 times a day.
IER: after using the tuning forks and Gemstones, have the client breathe into the feet area, press lightly on the feet on the out breath, repeat 2 times.
Reiki: Apply the Reiki with the hands over the stones for 15 minutes

Fertility
Tuning Forks: Balance Chakras and Organs, then use Selenium fork waving it over the reproductive area of the body, then seal in with Creation fork
Gems & Crystals: Aurauralite, Bloodstone, Amethyst, Pyrite, lay the stones on the Ovaries for 20 minutes 6 times a day.
IER: after using the tuning forks and Gemstones, have the client breathe into the reproductive area, press lightly on the reproductive area on the out breath, repeat 5 times
Reiki: Apply the Reiki with the hands over the stones for 15 minutes

Fever
Tuning Forks: Balance Chakras, then use Liver fork, Calcium fork, Oxygen fork for 5 minutes each fork then seal in with Creation fork
Gems & Crystals: Aurauralite, Azurite, Sugilite, Amethyst, Celestite, Tanzanite, Blue Tourmaline, Sapphire, Lavender Quartz, Purple Fluorite, Charoite, lay the stones on the forehead for 20 minutes.
IER: after using the tuning forks and Gemstones, have the client breathe into the forehead area, press lightly on the forehead area on the out breath, repeat 2 times.
Reiki: Apply the Reiki with the hands over the stones for 15 minutes

Fibroid Tumors & Cysts
Tuning Forks: Use the Stem Cell process Lymphatic process, and the Endocrine process, then seal with Creation fork
Gems & Crystals: Bloodstone, Emerald, Citrine, Golden Topaz, lay on area for 15 minutes 5 times per day.
IER: after using the tuning forks and Gemstones, have the client breathe into the forehead area, press lightly on the forehead area on the out breath, repeat 2 times.
Reiki: Apply the Reiki with the hands over the stones for 15 minutes

Flatulence
Tuning Forks: Use the Potassium fork and Stomach fork, waving over stomach area for 5 minutes each fork, then use Creation fork to seal in
Gems & Crystals: Emerald, Bloodstone lay on stomach area for 15 minutes.
IER: after using the tuning forks and Gemstones, have the client breathe into the bladder area, press lightly on the bladder area on the out breath, repeat 2 times.
Reiki: Apply the Reiki with the hands over the stones for 15 minutes

Flu
Tuning Forks: Balance Chakras and Organs, then use Oxygen fork, Circulation fork, Energy fork, Adrenal fork, use each fork for 5 minutes each then seal in with Creation fork

Gems & Crystals: Malachite, Morganite, Kunzite, Green Aventurine, Ruby, Hiddenite, Grossular Garnet, Green Jade, lay stones across the chest area for 15 minutes 3 times a day, until symptoms are gone.
IER: after using the tuning forks and Gemstones, have the client breathe into the chest/lung area, press lightly on the chest/lung area on the out breath, repeat 4 times.
Reiki: Apply the Reiki with the hands over the stones for 15 minutes

Fluid Retention
Tuning Forks: Balance Chakras and Organs, then use the Lymphatic process, and seal with Creation fork
Gems & Crystals: Bloodstone, Hemaite, Hiddenite, lay stones on the lower back just above buttocks for 20 minutes 3 times a day for 30 days.
IER: after using the tuning forks and Gemstones, have the client breathe into the stomach area, press lightly on the stomach area on the out breath, repeat 2 times.
Reiki: Apply the Reiki with the hands over the stones for 15 minutes

G

Gallstones
Tuning Forks: Use 3rd, 4th and 6th Chakra forks each for 5 minutes waving over the area, then seal in with Creation fork
Gems & Crystals: Amethyst, Celestite, Tanzanite, Blue Tourmaline, Sapphire, Lavender Quartz, Purple Fluorite, place stones over the Gallbladder area for 20 minutes 4 times a day for 20 days.
IER: after using the tuning forks and Gemstones, have the client breathe into the gallbladder area, press lightly on the gallbladder area on the out breath, repeat 3 times.
Reiki: Apply the Reiki with the hands over the stones for 15 minutes

Goiter
Tuning Forks: Balance Chakras then use Iodine fork, use fork for 10 minutes then seal with Creation fork
Gems & Crystals: Sodalite, Iolite, place stones on the area of the body for 15 minutes 3 times a day for 7 days.
IER: after using the tuning forks and Gemstones, have the client breathe into the affected area, press lightly on the affected area on the out breath, repeat 2 times.
Reiki: Apply the Reiki with the hands over the stones for 15 minutes

Gout
Tuning Forks: Balance Chakras, then use Manganese fork, using the fork on the joints, tendons for 10 minutes 3 times per day for 30 days (remember to seal in session with Creation fork)
Gems & Crystals: Chromite, lay the stone on the body area for 15 minutes 3 times a day for 30 days.
IER: after using the tuning forks and Gemstones, have the client breathe into the affected area, press lightly on the affected area on the out breath, repeat 2 times.
Reiki: Apply the Reiki with the hands over the stones for 15 minutes

Grave's Disease
Tuning Forks: Balance Chakras and Organs, then use Muscle fork specificly all over the body waving it for 20 minutes, then use the Nerve fork for 5 minutes waving it as well, then seal inwith Creation fork

Gems & Crystals: Tanzanite, Blue Tourmaline, Sapphire, Lavender Quartz, lay on body for 20 minutes 3 times a day for 60 days.
IER: after using the tuning forks and Gemstones, have the client breathe into the affected area, press lightly on the affected area on the out breath, repeat 2 times.
Reiki: Apply the Reiki with the hands over the stones for 15 minutes

H

Hair Loss
Tuning Forks: Balance the Chakras, then use Potassium fork and Copper fork placing stem on scalp for 10 minutes each for 2 times per day for 60 days
Gems & Crystals: Copper nuggets, place stones on top of head for 15 minutes 3 times a day.
IER: after using the tuning forks and Gemstones, have the client breathe into the crown of the head area, press lightly on the crown of the head area on the out breath, repeat 4 times.
Reiki: Apply the Reiki with the hands over the stones for 15 minutes

Hay Fever
Tuning Forks: Balance Chakras, and stength the Immune System by using the process described in the Lympathic and Endocrine Systems Booklets.
Gems & Crystals: Blue Topaz, Blue Tourmaline, Celestite, Indicolite, Blue Turquoise, Chrysocolla, Amazonite, Lapis Lazuli, Larimar, Sodalite, Iolite, place stones on the chest area for 15 minutes 3 times a day for 21 days.
IER: after using the tuning forks and Gemstones, have the client breathe into the sinus area, press lightly on the sinus area on the out breath, repeat 2 times.
Reiki: Apply the Reiki with the hands over the stones for 15 minutes

Headaches
Tuning Forks: See pain Relief Booklet and use Manganese fork
Gems & Crystals: Manganite, place stone on the forehead area for 15 minutes.
IER: after using the tuning forks and Gemstones, have the client breathe into the forehead area, press lightly on the forehead area on the out breath, repeat 2 times.
Reiki: Apply the Reiki with the hands over the stones for 15 minutes

Hearing Problems
Tuning Forks: Balance Chakras and Organs then use the Nerve fork, Oxygen fork under the ear lobe area for 5 minute each fork, then seal in with Creation fork
Gems & Crystals: Amethyst, Celestite, Tanzanite, Blue Tourmaline, Sapphire, Lavender Quartz, Purple Fluorite, Charoite, Sodalite, lay stones in a circle around the ear for 20 minutes 2 times a
IER: after using the tuning forks and Gemstones, have the client breathe into the ears, press lightly on the temples area on the out breath, repeat 2 times a day for 40 days.
Reiki: Apply the Reiki with the hands over the stones for 15 minutes

Heartburn
Tuning Forks: Use Stomach fork, Adrenals fork, Liver fork, and Colon fork, use each fork for 5 minutes then seal in with Creation fork
Gems & Crystals: Bloodstone, Yellow Tourmaline, Tiger's Eye, Heliodor, Rutilated Quartz, Amber, Sunstone, Malachite, Peridot, Emerald, lay stones on the stomach area in a circular pattern for 20 minutes every 2 hours.
IER: after using the tuning forks and Gemstones, have the client breathe into the abdomen area, press lightly on the abdomen area on the out breath, repeat 2 times.
Reiki: Apply the Reiki with the hands over the stones for 15 minutes

Heart Problems
Tuning Forks: Balance Chakras, then use Blood fork, Adrenal fork, Circulation fork, Iodine fork, Oxygen fork each for 5 minutes waving over the chest area, then seal in with Creation fork
Gems & Crystals: Rose Quartz, Pink Tourmaline, Rubellite, Rhodochrosite, Emerald, Green Tourmaline, Malachite, Morganite, Kunzite, Green Aventurine, Ruby, Hiddenite, Grossular Garnet, Green Jade, place the stones in a medicine wheel, with the Green Jade as the center piece of the wheel, leave the wheel in place for 20 minutes, do 3 times a day.
IER: after using the tuning forks and Gemstones, have the client breathe into the chest area, press lightly on the chest/heart area on the out breath, repeat 2 times.
Reiki: Apply the Reiki with the hands over the stones for 15 minutes

Hemmorrhoids
Tuning Forks: Use Colon fork, Blood fork, 1st, 2nd, 3rd Chakra forks, wave over the area for 10 minutes each day (2 minutes per fork), then seal in with Creation fork
Gems & Crystals: Golden Topaz, Green-Yellow Tourmaline, Tiger's Eye, Heliodor, Rutilated Quartz, Amber, Sunstone, Malachite, Peridot, Emerald, lay the stones in a circle on a pillow, then sit on the stones for 15 minutes.
IER: after using the tuning forks and Gemstones, have the client breathe into the buttocks area, press lightly on the buttocks area on the out breath, repeat 2 times.
Reiki: Apply the Reiki with the hands over the stones for 15 minutes

Hepatitis
Tuning Forks: Balance Chakras and Organs, then use protocol on the Immune system
Gems & Crystals: Cornelian, Garnet, Ruby, Cuprite, Black Tourmaline, Smoky Quartz, Onyx, Agate, Black Obsidian, Hematite, Fire Agate, Ametrine, place the stones on the chest for 10 minutes 2 times a day for 14 days.
IER: after using the tuning forks and Gemstones, have the client breathe into the chest area, press lightly on the chest area on the out breath, repeat 2 times.
Reiki: Apply the Reiki with the hands over the stones for 15 minutes

Herpes
Tuning Forks: Balance Chakras and Organs then boost Immune sytems with Lynpathic and Endocrine proceedures.
Gems & Crystals: Bloodstone, Hematite, Aurauralite, Pyrite, hold the stones one each over area for 5 minutes each stone 2 times per day.
IER: after using the tuning forks and Gemstones, have the client breathe into the affected area, press lightly on the afftected area on the out breath, repeat 2 times.
Reiki: Apply the Reiki with the hands over the stones for 15 minutes

High Blood Pressure
Tuning Forks: See pain Relief Booklet
Gems & Crystals: Bloodstone, Nephrite, Kunzite, Prehnite, Chrysoprase, Rhodonite, Moldavite, Prasiolite, Watermelon Tourmaline, place stones on the heart area for 15 minutes, 6 times a day.
IER: after using the tuning forks and Gemstones, have the client breathe into the heart area, press lightly on the heart area on the out breath, repeat 2 times.
Reiki: Apply the Reiki with the hands over the stones for 15 minutes

Hyperglycemia

Tuning Forks: Use 1st, 2nd and 3rd Chakra forks, then use Adrenal fork, Liver fork, Stomach fork each for 10 minutes, then seal with Creation fork
Gems & Crystals: Aragonite, Orange Calcite, Selenite, Zircon, place stones on the liver area for 15 minutes 2 times a day.
IER: after using the tuning forks and Gemstones, have the client breathe into the liver area, press lightly on the liver area on the out breath, repeat 2 times.
Reiki: Apply the Reiki with the hands over the stones for 15 minutes

I

Immune Problems
Tuning Forks: Use protocols in Lympathic and Endocrine booklets
Gems & Crystals: Cornelian, Garnet, Ruby, Cuprite, Black Tourmaline, Smoky Quartz, Onyx, Agate, Black Obsidian, Hematite, place the stones on the spots indicated in the Lymphatic booklet 2 times a day.
IER: after using the tuning forks and Gemstones, have the client breathe into the areas indicated in the booklet, press lightly on each area in the Lymphatic booklet on the out breath, repeat 2 times.
Reiki: Apply the Reiki with the hands over the stones for 15 minutes

Impatience
Tuning Forks: Balance Chakras, then use Om fork, Manganese fork, and Adrenal fork waving them over the body for 5 minutes each for then seal inwith Creation fork
Gems & Crystals: Aurauralite, wear the pendant for several weeks.
IER: after using the tuning forks and Gemstones, have the client breathe into the forehead area, press lightly on the forehead area on the out breath, repeat 3 times.
Reiki: Apply the Reiki with the hands over the stones for 15 minutes

Impotence
Tuning Forks: Balance fork then use use protocol in Endrocrine boklet for Testes area
Gems & Crystals: Ametrine, Blood Stone, Nephrite, place stones on Endocrine point as described in booklet, 2 times a day for 14 days.
IER: after using the tuning forks and Gemstones, have the client breathe into the Endocrine points in the booklet, press lightly on the points shown in the Endocrine booklet on the out breath, repeat the process 2 times, for 14 days.
Reiki: Apply the Reiki with the hands over the stones for 15 minutes

Incontinence
Tuning Forks: Balance the Chakras, then use Om fork, Bladder fork, Muscle fork, Kidney fork, waving it over the area for 5 minutes each fork 2 times a day for 21 days.
Gems & Crystals: Golden Topaz, Golden Beryl, Aragonite, Orange Calcite, Selenite, Zircon, Sunstone, Tiger's Eye, Heliodor, place stones under the pelvis area with client laying on stones for 20 minutes 2 times a day.
IER: after using the tuning forks and Gemstones, have the client breathe into the pelvis area, press lightly on the pelvis area on the out breath, repeat 2 times.
Reiki: Apply the Reiki with the hands over the stones for 15 minutes

Indigestion
Tuning Forks: Balance Chakras, then use Om fork, Stomach fork, Calcium fork, wave fork over the solar plexus area for 5 minutes each fork, then seal with Creation fork.

Gems & Crystals: Citrine, Golden Topaz, Green-Yellow Tourmaline, Amber, place stones on the stomach in a clockwise pattern with Citrine at 12, Golden topaz at 3pm and so on, for 15 minutes.
IER: after using the tuning forks and Gemstones, have the client breathe into the abdomen area, press lightly on the abdomen area on the out breath, repeat 2 times.
Reiki: Apply the Reiki with the hands over the stones for 15 minutes

Infection
Tuning Forks: Balance Chakras, then use Adrenal fork, Zinc fork, for 5 minutes each fork over the area, then use stones and seal with Creation fork
Gems & Crystals: Bloodstone, Aurauralite, place on or near area for 10 minutes 3 times a day for 7 days.
IER: after using the tuning forks and Gemstones, have the client breathe into the affected area, press lightly on the forehead area on the out breath, repeat 2 times.
Reiki: Apply the Reiki with the hands over the stones for 15 minutes

Infertility
Tuning Forks: Balance Chakras and Organs, then use Om fork, Selenium fork, Zinc fork over reproductive area for 5 minutes each fork 2 times per day, then use stone's then, seal in with Creation fork
Gems & Crystals: Cornelian, Garnet, Ruby, Cuprite, Black Tourmaline, Smoky Quartz, Onyx, Agate, Black Obsidian, Hematite, Fire Agate, Ametrine, Blood Stone, lay stones on the Ovaries area for 15 minutes 6 times a day.
IER: after using the tuning forks and Gemstones, have the client breathe into the Ovaries area, press lightly on the Ovaries area on the out breath, repeat 2 times.
Reiki: Apply the Reiki with the hands over the stones for 15 minutes

Inflammation
Tuning Forks: Use 3rd, 4th and 5th Chakra forks, then use Stem Cell protocols.
Gems & Crystals: Indicolite, Blue Turquoise, Chrysocolla, Amazonite, Lapis Lazuli, Larimar, Sodalite, Iolite, Kyanite, place stones on or near area for 15 minutes 5 times a day for 7 days.
IER: after using the tuning forks and Gemstones, have the client breathe into the inflamed area, press lightly on the forehead area on the out breath, repeat 2 times.
Reiki: Apply the Reiki with the hands over the stones for 15 minutes

Insomnia
Tuning Forks: Use 3rd, 6th, and 7th Chakra forks, then use the energy fork hold the tuning fork by the stem/handle and place the tip of the handle on your tailbone. Lastly, place the stem of the fork on the base of the skull, do this for 5 minutes on each spot, then seal in session with the Creation fork
Gems & Crystals: Moonstone, Lavender Quartz, Rutilated Quartz, Diamond, White Topaz, place stones on the forehead for 25 minutes before bed.
IER: after using the tuning forks and Gemstones, have the client breathe into the forehead area, press lightly on the forehead area on the out breath, repeat 2 times.
Reiki: Apply the Reiki with the hands over the stones for 15 minutes

Irritable Bowel Syndrome
Tuning Forks: Balance the chakras, then use the Colon fork, Nerve fork, Stomach fork use each fork for 5 minutes each then seal in with the Creation fork

Gems & Crystals: Cornelian, Garnet, Ruby, Cuprite, Black Tourmaline, Smoky Quartz, Onyx, Agate, Black Obsidian, Hematite, Fire Agate, Ametrine, Blood Stone, Nephrite, place stones on a pillow in a circlular fashion then sit on pillow for 30 minutes.
IER: after using the tuning forks and Gemstones, have the client breathe into the lower abdomen area, press lightly on the lower abdomen area on the out breath, repeat 2 times.
Reiki: Apply the Reiki with the hands over the stones for 15 minutes

J

Jaundice
Tuning Forks: Balance the Chakras, then Blood fork, then use the Stem Cell procedure.
Gems & Crystals: No specific stones recommended
IER: after using the tuning forks and Gemstones, have the client breathe into the forehead area, press lightly on the forehead area on the out breath, repeat 2 times.

Joint Problems
Tuning Forks: Balance the Chakras then use, the Nerve fork, Oxygen fork, Circulation fork, Bone fork, use each fork for 5 minutes then seal with Creation fork
Gems & Crystals: Black Obsidian, Hematite, Orange Calcite, Selenite, Zircon, Citrine, Golden Topaz, lay the stones on the join areas for 15 minutes 3 times a day.
IER: after using the tuning forks and Gemstones, have the client breathe into the affected area, press lightly on the affected area on the out breath, repeat 2 times.
Reiki: Apply the Reiki with the hands over the stones for 15 minutes

K

Kidney Problems
Tuning Forks: Balance the Chakras, then use the Kidney fork for 5 minutes, then use the process in the Endocrine Booklet
Gems & Crystals: Bloodstone, Black Obsidian, Hematite, Fire Agate, Ametrine, lay stone on the Kidney area for 20 minutes 3 times a day for 20 days.
IER: after using the tuning forks and Gemstones, have the client breathe into the Kidney area, press lightly on the Kidney area on the out breath, repeat 2 times.
Reiki: Apply the Reiki with the hands over the stones for 15 minutes

Kidney Stones
Tuning Forks: Balance the Chakras then use the protocol from the Lymphatic & Endocrine Booklets
Gems & Crystals: Bloodstone, Black Obsidian, Hematite, Fire Agate, Ametrine, lay stone on the Kidney area for 20 minutes 3 times a day for 20 days.
IER: after using the tuning forks and Gemstones, have the client breathe into the Kidney area, press lightly on the Kidney area on the out breath, repeat 3 times.
Reiki: Apply the Reiki with the hands over the stones for 15 minutes

Knee Problems
Tuning Forks: Balance the Chakras, then use the Nerve fork, Oxygen fork, Circulation fork, use each for 10 minutes on the knee area, then seal with Creation fork
Gems & Crystals: Bloodstone, Hematite, Black Tourmaline, Smoky Quartz, Onyx, Agate, lay stones on the knee for 15 minutes 4 times a day for 21 days.
IER: after using the tuning forks and Gemstones, have the client breathe into the Knee area, press lightly on the Knee on the out breath, repeat 2 times.
Reiki: Apply the Reiki with the hands over the stones for 15 minutes

L

Laryngitis
Tuning Forks: Use 5th Chakra fork, 4th Chakra fork, and 6th Chakra fork, then use Oxygen, Circulation fork, each for 5 minutes then seal with Creation fork
Gems & Crystals: Indicolite, Blue Turquoise, Chrysocolla, Amazonite, Lapis Lazuli, Larimar, Sodalite, place the stones on the throat area for 20 minutes, 2 times a day.
IER: after using the tuning forks and Gemstones, have the client breathe into the throat area, press lightly on the throat area on the out breath, repeat 2 times.
Reiki: Apply the Reiki with the hands over the stones for 15 minutes

Leg Problems
Tuning Forks: Balance Chakras, then use Nerve fork, Oxygen fork, Circulation fork, wave over leg area for 10 minutes each fork then seal with Creation fork
Gems & Crystals: Bloodstone, Lapis Lazuli, Amazonite, Hematite, Black Tourmaline, lay on the leg starting at the knee downward towards the ankle for 20 minutes 3 times a day for 21 days.
IER: after using the tuning forks and Gemstones, have the client breathe into the leg area, press lightly on the leg area on the out breath, repeat 2 times.
Reiki: Apply the Reiki with the hands over the stones for 15 minutes

Lethargy
Tuning Forks: Balance Chakras then use Iron fork wave over entire body for 15 minutes, then seal with Creation fork
Gems & Crystals: Tanzanite, Blue Tourmaline, Sapphire, Lavender Quartz, Purple Fluorite, place the stones on forehead over the third eye area for 5 minutes each stone for 7 days.
IER: after using the tuning forks and Gemstones, have the client breathe into the forehead/third eye area, press lightly on the forehead/third eye area on the out breath, repeat 2 times.
Reiki: Apply the Reiki with the hands over the stones for 15 minutes

Leukemia
Tuning Forks: Balance Chakras and Organs, then use Bone fork, Blood fork, also use Stem Cell process, Lymphatic process, and Endocrine process.
Gems & Crystals: Tanzanite, Blue Tourmaline, Sapphire, Lavender Quartz, Purple Fluorite, Tiger's Eye, Heliodor, Rutilated Quartz, Amber, Sunstone, lay stones on the stomach area in a circular method with the Amber stone as the center for 20 minutes for 21 days.
IER: after using the tuning forks and Gemstones, have the client breathe into the Abdomen area, press lightly on the abdomen area on the out breath, repeat 2 times.
Reiki: Apply the Reiki with the hands over the stones for 15 minutes

Liver Problems
Tuning Forks: Balance Chakras, the use Blood fork, Stomach fork, Liver fork, Adrenals fork, use each fork for 5 minutes, then seal in with Creation fork
Gems & Crystals: Amber, Sunstone, Tanzanite, Blue Tourmaline, Sapphire, Lavender Quartz, lay stones on the liver area for 15 minutes for 7 days.
IER: after using the tuning forks and Gemstones, have the client breathe into the Liver area, press lightly on the Liver area on the out breath, repeat 2 times.
Reiki: Apply the Reiki with the hands over the stones for 15 minutes

Lou Gehrig's Disease

Tuning Forks: Balance Chakras, then use Nerve fork, Brain fork, on the temples of each side of the head for 5 minutes each, the use the Muscle fork on the back for 10 minutes waving over the area, then seal in with Creation fork
Gems & Crystals: Azurite, Sugilite, Amethyst, Celestite, Tanzanite, Blue Tourmaline, Sapphire, Lavender Quartz, Purple Fluorite, Charoite, Sodalite, Iolite, Amethyst, Howlite, Moonstone, Lavender Quartz, Rutilated Quartz, lay stones on the body starting with the throat-Amethyst, then chest area with Celestite, Tanzanite, Blue Tourmaline, Sapphire, Lavender Quartz, Purple Fluorite, Charoite, then the stomach area with remainder of the stones, for 20 minutes 5 times a day.
IER: after using the tuning forks and Gemstones, have the client breathe into the throat area visualizing the energy going down to the abdomen area then, press lightly on the abdomen area on the out breath, repeat 2 times.
Reiki: Apply the Reiki with the hands over the stones for 15 minutes

Lumps

Tuning Forks: Balance Chakras, then do the Lymphatic process and Endocrine process, then seal in with Creation fork
Gems & Crystals: Bloodstone, Amethyst, Celestite, Lavender Quartz, Howlite, Moonstone, place the stones on the affected area for 15 minutes 3 times a day for 17 days.
IER: after using the tuning forks and Gemstones, have the client breathe into the affected area, press lightly on the affected area on the out breath, repeat 2 times.
Reiki: Apply the Reiki with the hands over the stones for 15 minutes

Lung Problems

Tuning Forks: Balance fork, then use Lung fork, Iodine fork, Calcium fork for 10 minutes waving each over the chest area, then seal in with Creation fork
Gems & Crystals: Apophyllite, Aquamarine, Blue Lace Agate, Blue Topaz, Blue Tourmaline, Celestite, Indicolite, place the stones on the lung area for 15 minutes, 3 times a day.
IER: after using the tuning forks and Gemstones, have the client breathe into the chest/lung area, press lightly on the chest/lung area on the out breath, repeat 2 times.
Reiki: Apply the Reiki with the hands over the stones for 15 minutes

Lupus

Tuning Forks: Balance Chakras, then use Stem Cell process, Lymphatic process and Endocrine process
Gems & Crystals: Indicolite, Celestite, Lavender Quartz, Howlite, lay over the chest area for 15 minutes for 6 days.
IER: after using the tuning forks and Gemstones, have the client breathe into the chest area, press lightly on the chest area on the out breath, repeat 2 times.
Reiki: Apply the Reiki with the hands over the stones for 15 minutes

Lyme Disease

Tuning Forks: Use the Lymphatic process (see Tuning Fork Manual), use the Nerve fork for 10 minutes, on areas where there is pain, then use the following gemstones in the same area; quartz crystal, bloodstone, agate, then seal the session with the Creation tuning fork.
Gems & Crystals: Quartz crystal, bloodstone, agate, then seal the session with the Creation tuning fork.
IER: after using the tuning forks and Gemstones, have the client breathe into the Lymphatic areas, press lightly on the Lymphatic points on the out breath, repeat 2 times on each point for 21 days.
Reiki: Apply the Reiki with the hands over the stones for 15 minutes

Lymph Problems
Tuning Forks: Balance the Chakras and Organs, then do the Lymphatic process.
Gems & Crystals: Bloostone, Lavender Quartz, Howlite, Purple Fluorite, Charoite, Moonstone, Lavender Quartz, lay the stones on the Lymphatic System- use chart in booklet of Tuning Fork Lymphatic process for 20 minutes.
IER: after using the tuning forks and Gemstones, have the client breathe into the lymph node areas, press lightly on the lymph node areas on the out breath, repeat 2 times on each node point.
Reiki: Apply the Reiki with the hands over the stones for 15 minutes

Lymphoma
Tuning Forks: Balance the Chakras and Organs, then do the Lymphatic and Endocrine process
Gems & Crystals: Bloostone, Lavender Quartz, Howlite, Purple Fluorite, Charoite, Moonstone, Lavender Quartz, lay the stones on the Lymphatic System- use chart in booklet of Tuning Fork Lymphatic process for 20 minutes.
IER: after using the tuning forks and Gemstones, have the client breathe into the Kidney area, press lightly on the Kidney area on the out breath, repeat 2 times.
Reiki: Apply the Reiki with the hands over the stones for 15 minutes

M

Measles
Tuning Forks: Balance Chakra and Organs, then use Creation fork to seal in session
Gems & Crystals: Amber, Moonstone, Cornelian, Citrine, Golden Topaz, Golden Beryl, Aragonite, Orange Calcite, Selenite, Zircon, lay the stones on the affected area for 15 minutes 3 times a day.
IER: after using the tuning forks and Gemstones, have the client breathe into the affected area, press lightly on the affected area on the out breath, repeat 2 times.
Reiki: Apply the Reiki with the hands over the stones for 15 minutes

Memory
Tuning Forks: Balance the Chakras, then use Brain fork, Iron fork each for 5 minutes waving over the head area, then seal in with Creation fork.
Gems & Crystals: Amethyst, Howlite, Moonstone, Lavender Quartz, Rutilated Quartz, Diamond, White Topaz, place the stones on the forehead for 15 minutes 2 times a day for 21 days.
IER: after using the tuning forks and Gemstones, have the client breathe into the forehead area, press lightly on the forehead area on the out breath, repeat 2 times.
Reiki: Apply the Reiki with the hands over the stones for 15 minutes

Menopausal Problems
Tuning Forks: Balance Chakras and Organs then do Endocrine process.
Gems & Crystals: Black Tourmaline, Smoky Quartz, Onyx, Agate, Black Obsidian, Hematite, Cornelian, Garnet, Ruby, Cuprite, Aragonite, Orange Calcite, Selenite, Zircon, lay stones on the lower abdomen area for 15 minutes 4 times a day, for 6 days.
IER: after using the tuning forks and Gemstones, have the client breathe into the lower abdomen area, press lightly on the lower abdomen area on the out breath, repeat 2 times.
Reiki: Apply the Reiki with the hands over the stones for 15 minutes

Mental Confusion

Tuning Forks: Balance Chakras and Organs, then use Manganese fork, Iodine fork, Potassium fork for 10 minutes each waving over the head area, then seal in with the Creation fork.
Gems & Crystals: Ametrine, Clear Quartz Crystal, Amethyst, Lavender Quartz, Purple Fluorite, lay the stones on the forehead for 15 minutes 2 time a day for 6 days.
IER: after using the tuning forks and Gemstones, have the client breathe into their forehead area, press lightly on the forehead on the out breath, repeat 2 times.
Reiki: Apply the Reiki with the hands over the stones for 15 minutes

Migraines
Tuning Forks: See Pain Relief Booklet
Gems & Crystals: Manganite, Bloodstone, place stones on the forehead area for 15 minutes.
IER: after using the tuning forks and Gemstones, have the client breathe into the lower abdomen area, press lightly on the forehead/temple area on the out breath, repeat 2 times.
Reiki: Apply the Reiki with the hands over the stones for 15 minutes

Mononucleosis
Tuning Forks: Balance the Chakras and Organs, then do the Lymphatic process.
Gems & Crystals: Malachite, Morganite, Kunzite, Green Aventurine, Ruby, Hiddenite, Grossular Garnet, Green Jade, place stones on the chest area for 12 minutes 3 times a day for 19 days.
IER: after using the tuning forks and Gemstones, have the client breathe into the chest area, press lightly on the lower chest area on the out breath, repeat 2 times.
Reiki: Apply the Reiki with the hands over the stones for 15 minutes

Motion Sickness
Tuning Forks: Balance the Chakras and Organs, then use Circulation fork, Oxygen fork waving over the head area for 10 minutes, then seal in with Creation fork.
Gems & Crystals: Indicolite, Blue Turquoise, Chrysocolla, Amazonite, Lapis Lazuli, Larimar, Sodalite, Iolite, Kyanite, place on the forehead for 15 minutes.
IER: after using the tuning forks and Gemstones, have the client breathe into the forehead area, press lightly on the forehead on the out breath, repeat 3 times.
Reiki: Apply the Reiki with the hands over the stones for 15 minutes

Multiple Sclerosis
Tuning Forks: Use Intuitive Emotional Release process
Gems & Crystals: Cornelian, Garnet, Ruby, Cuprite, Black Tourmaline, Smoky Quartz, Onyx, Agate, Black Obsidian, Hematite, Fire Agate, Ametrine, Blood Stone, Nephrite, lay stones on the entire body starting with the throat area working down to the ankles, do for 21 days 15 minutes at a time.
IER: after using the tuning forks and Gemstones, have the client breathe into the ankles, press lightly on the ankles on the out breath, repeat 3 times.
Reiki: Apply the Reiki with the hands over the stones for 15 minutes

Muscular Dystrophy
Tuning Forks: Balance Chakras and Organs then use Nerve fork for 20 minutes over the entire body by waving it 6 inches above the body, then seal in with the Creation fork
Gems & Crystals: Cuprite, Black Tourmaline, Smoky Quartz, Onyx, Agate, Black Obsidian, Hematite, Fire Agate, Ametrine, Blood Stone, Nephrite, lay stones on the chest and abdomen area for 15 minutes 3 times a day.
IER: after using the tuning forks and Gemstones, have the client breathe into the chest & abdomen area, press lightly on the abdomen on the out breath, repeat 3 times.

Reiki: Apply the Reiki with the hands over the stones for 15 minutes

N

Nausea
Tuning Forks: Use 1st, 2nd, 3rd, and 6th Chakra forks, then use Stomach fork for 5 minutes over stomach area, then seal in with Creation fork.
Gems & Crystals: Citrine, Golden Topaz, Green-Yellow Tourmaline, Tiger's Eye, Heliodor, Rutilated Quartz, Amber, Sunstone, lay stones on the stomach are for 15 minutes.
IER: after using the tuning forks and Gemstones, have the client breathe into the abdomen area, press lightly on the abdomen on the out breath, repeat 3 times.
Reiki: Apply the Reiki with the hands over the stones for 15 minutes

Neck Problems
Tuning Forks: Balance Chakras, then use Nerve fork and Muscle fork, on neck for 15 minutes, placing stem on Neck sliding along neck from shoulder (trapezius muscle) to head/Cranial area.
Gems & Crystals: Azurite, Sugilite, Amethyst, Celestite, Tanzanite, Blue Tourmaline, Sapphire, Lavender Quartz, Purple Fluorite, place the stones on the throat area for 10 minutes 5 times a day for 7 days.
IER: after using the tuning forks and Gemstones, have the client breathe into the throat area, press lightly on the abdomen on the out breath, repeat 2 times.
Reiki: Apply the Reiki with the hands over the stones for 15 minutes

Neuralgia
Tuning Forks: Use 3rd, 5th, and 6th Chakra fork, for 5 minutes each then use the Phosphorus fork for 10 minutes, then seal in with Creation fork.
Gems & Crystals: Azurite, Amethyst, Celestite, Tanzanite, Blue Tourmaline, Sapphire, Lavender Quartz, Purple Fluorite, Amazonite, Lapis Lazuli, Larimar, Sodalite, Iolite, Kyanite, place the stones on the left side of the body from the arm pit to the middle of the stomach, for 20 minutes 2 times a day.
IER: after using the tuning forks and Gemstones, have the client breathe into the abdomen area, press lightly on the abdomen on the out breath, repeat 3 times.
Reiki: Apply the Reiki with the hands over the stones for 15 minutes

Nose Problems
Tuning Fork: Balance Chakras, then use Adrenal fork, Muscle fork, for 5 minutes each then seal in with Creation fork.
Gems & Crystals: Blue Tourmaline, Sapphire, Lapis Lazuli, Kyanite, hold the stones on the nose one stone at a time, 5 minutes each stone for 3 days.
IER: after using the tuning forks and Gemstones, have the client breathe into the sinus area, press lightly on the abdomen on the out breath, repeat 3 times.
Reiki: Apply the Reiki with the hands over the stones for 15 minutes

Numbness
Tuning Forks: See pain relief booklet and use Phosphorus fork for 10 minutes waving over area of numbness, then seal with Creation fork.
Gems & Crystals: Bloodstone, Aurauralite, lay stones on the area of numbness for 15 minutes 4 times a day for 21 days.
IER: after using the tuning forks and Gemstones, have the client breathe into the affected area, press lightly on the abdomen on the out breath, repeat 4 times.
Reiki: Apply the Reiki with the hands over the stones for 15 minutes

O

Obesity
Tuning Forks: Balance Chakras, then use Fat Cell fork, Muscle fork with massage for 30 minutes twice a week, seal in session with Creation fork.
Gems & Crystals: Blood stone, Golden Beryl, Aragonite, Orange Calcite, lay the stones on the abdomen for 20 minutes 7 times a day, for 30 days.
IER: after using the tuning forks and Gemstones, have the client breathe into the abdomen area, press lightly on the abdomen on the out breath, repeat 3 times.
Reiki: Apply the Reiki with the hands over the stones for 15 minutes

Osteoporosis
Tuning Forks: See Pain Relief Booklet, and use Copper fork for 10 minutes each day, and seal in session with Creation fork.
Gems & Crystals: Bloodstone, Kunzite, Green Aventurine, Ruby, lay on affected areas for 20 minutes each day.
IER: after using the tuning forks and Gemstones, have the client breathe into the affected area, press lightly on the abdomen on the out breath, repeat 3 times.
Reiki: Apply the Reiki with the hands over the stones for 15 minutes

Ovarian Cancer
Tuning Forks: Balance the Chakras, then use Endocrine process, and then use Sekheim fork with the Creation for 20 minutes each day.
Gems & Crystals: Amber, Sunstone, Malachite, Cornelian, Garnet, Ruby, Cuprite, lay on the body between stomach and pelvic area in circle pattern for 20 minutes a day.
IER: after using the tuning forks and Gemstones, have the client breathe into the abdomen area, press lightly on the abdomen on the out breath, repeat 3 times.
Reiki: Apply the Reiki with the hands over the stones for 15 minutes

P

Pain
Tuning Forks: See Pain Relief Booklet and use Calcium fork and Potassium fork for 10 minutes each fork then seal with Creation fork.
Gems & Crystals: Aurauralite, Bloodstone, lay the stones on the area of pain for 30 minutes.
IER: after using the tuning forks and Gemstones, have the client breathe into the pain area, press lightly on the abdomen on the out breath, repeat 3 times.
Reiki: Apply the Reiki with the hands over the stones for 15 minutes

Pancreatic Problems
Tuning Forks: Balance forks, and then use Pancreas fork for 15 minutes, then seal in with Creation fork.
Gems & Crystals: Aurauralite, Bloodstone, Golden Beryl, Aragonite, Orange Calcite, lay the stones over the area for 15 minutes 2 times a day.
IER: after using the tuning forks and Gemstones, have the client breathe into the pancreas area, press lightly on the pancreas on the out breath, repeat 3 times.
Reiki: Apply the Reiki with the hands over the stones for 15 minutes

Panic Attack
Tuning Forks: Balance Chakras and Organs, then use Oxygen fork waving it over the entire body for 10 minutes, then seal in with Creation fork

Gems & Crystals: Put Aurauralite and Pyrite at the head of the table, then place on the stomach, Yellow Tourmaline, Tiger's Eye, Heliodor, for 15 minutes, 3 times a day, for 21 days.
IER: after using the tuning forks and Gemstones, have the client breathe into the abdomen area, press lightly on the abdomen on the out breath, repeat 3 times.
Reiki: Apply the Reiki with the hands over the stones for 15 minutes

Parkinson's
Tuning Forks: Balance the Chakras and Organs, then use DNA fork, Nerve fork, Circulation fork, Oxygen fork, using each for 5 minutes, then sealing in with Creation fork.
Gems & Crystals: Amethyst, Howlite, Moonstone, Lavender Quartz, Rutilated Quartz, Apophyllite, Aquamarine, Blue Lace Agate, Blue Topaz, Blue Tourmaline, Celestite, Indicolite, Blue Turquoise, Chrysocolla, Amazonite, Lapis Lazuli, Diamond, place the stones on the chest to the stomach area in a figure 8 pattern, for 20 minutes, 3 times a day for 60 days.
IER: after using the tuning forks and Gemstones, have the client breathe into the chest area, press lightly on the abdomen on the out breath, repeat 3 times.
Reiki: Apply the Reiki with the hands over the stones for 15 minutes

Psoriasis
Tuning Forks: Balance the Chakra, then use the Oxygen fork, Circulation fork, and Nerve fork, use each fork for 5 minutes, then seal in with the Creation fork.
Gems & Crystals: Aurauralite, and Bloodstone, lay stones on the affected area, for 20 minutes 3 times a day for 16 days.
IER: after using the tuning forks and Gemstones, have the client breathe into the affected area, press lightly on the affected on the out breath, repeat 3 times.
Reiki: Apply the Reiki with the hands over the stones for 15 minutes

Q

R

Restlessness
Tuning Forks: Balance Chakras and Organs then use Iodine fork, Potassium fork, Oxygen fork, each for 5 minutes, then seal in with Creation fork.
Gems & Crystals: Smoky Quartz, Onyx, Agate, Black Obsidian, Hematite, Fire Agate, Blood Stone, Nephrite, Amber, Moonstone, Cornelian, Citrine, Golden Topaz, Golden Beryl, Aragonite, Selenite, Zircon, lay the stones on the upper back for 20 minutes, 3 times a day for 21 days.
IER: after using the tuning forks and Gemstones, have the client breathe into the upper back area, press lightly on the upper back on the out breath, repeat 3 times.
Reiki: Apply the Reiki with the hands over the stones for 15 minutes

Respiratory Aliments
Tuning Forks: Balance Chakras and Organs then use Zinc fork, Phosphorus fork, Copper fork, use each fork for 6 minutes each then seal in with Creation fork.
Gems & Crystals: Nephrite, Kunzite, Prehnite, Chrysoprase, Rhodonite, Moldavite, Prasiolite, lay the stones on the upper chest area for 20 minutes 3 times a day for 20 days.
IER: after using the tuning forks and Gemstones, have the client breathe into the upper chest area, press lightly on the upper chest on the out breath, repeat 3 times.
Reiki: Apply the Reiki with the hands over the stones for 15 minutes

Rheumatism
Tuning Forks: Balance Chakras, then use Bone fork, Kidney fork, Oxygen fork, Lung fork, Circulation fork, and the Nerve fork, use each for 10 minutes then seal with Creation fork.
Gems & Crystals: Bloodstone, Kunzite, Green Aventurine, Ruby, lay on affected areas for 20 minutes each day.
IER: after using the tuning forks and Gemstones, have the client breathe into the affected area, press lightly on the affected on the out breath, repeat 3 times.
Reiki: Apply the Reiki with the hands over the stones for 15 minutes

S

Sciatica
Tuning Forks: See Pain Relief Booklet
Gems & Crystals: Aurauralite, Bloodstone, Kunzite, Green Aventurine, Ruby, lay on affected areas for 20 minutes each day.
IER: after using the tuning forks and Gemstones, have the client breathe into the affected area, press lightly on the affected on the out breath, repeat 3 times.
Reiki: Apply the Reiki with the hands over the stones for 15 minutes

Seasickness
Tuning Forks: Balance the Chakras and Organs then use the Oxygen fork, then seal in with the Creation fork
Gems & Crystals: Bloodstone, Kunzite, Tiger's Eye, Heliodor, Rutilated Quartz, Amber, hold these stones over the stomach with each hand for 20 minutes.
IER: after using the tuning forks and Gemstones, have the client breathe into the abdomen area, press lightly on the abdomen on the out breath, repeat 3 times.
Reiki: Apply the Reiki with the hands over the stones for 15 minutes

Seizures
Tuning Forks: Balance the Chakras and the Organs and then use the Nerve fork for 25 minutes, then seal in with the Creation fork.
Gems & Crystals: Ametrine, Clear Quartz Crystal, Amethyst, Howlite, Moonstone, Lavender Quartz, Rutilated Quartz, lay the stones on the forehead for 15 minutes 4 times a day for 15 days.
IER: after using the tuning forks and Gemstones, have the client breathe into the forehead area, press lightly on the abdomen on the out breath, repeat 3 times.
Reiki: Apply the Reiki with the hands over the stones for 15 minutes

Shingles
Tuning Forks: Balance the Chakras and Organs, and then use the Nerve fork, DNA fork and use the Stem Cell process.
Gems & Crystals: Smoky Quartz, Onyx, Agate, Black Obsidian, Hematite, Fire Agate, Blood Stone, Nephrite, Amber, Moonstone, Cornelian, Citrine, Golden Topaz, Golden Beryl, Aragonite, Selenite, Zircon, lay these stones on the affected area for 20 minutes, 2 times a day for 15 days.
IER: after using the tuning forks and Gemstones, have the client breathe into the affected area, press lightly on the affected on the out breath, repeat 3 times.
Reiki: Apply the Reiki with the hands over the stones for 15 minutes

Shoulder Problems
Tuning Forks: Balance the Chakras, and use the Nerve fork (see Pain Relief Booklet) for 15 minutes gliding the stem of the fork along the shoulder.

Gems & Crystals: Azurite, Sugilite, Amethyst, Celestite, Tanzanite, Blue Tourmaline, Sapphire, Lavender Quartz, Purple Fluorite, Charoite, place these stones on the shoulder area for 20 minutes 3 times a day for 6 days.
IER: after using the tuning forks and Gemstones, have the client breathe into the shoulder area, press lightly on the shoulder on the out breath, repeat 3 times.
Reiki: Apply the Reiki with the hands over the stones for 15 minutes

Skin Problems
Tuning Forks: Balance the Chakras and Organs and then use the Copper fork for 15 minutes over the area, and seal with the Creation fork.
Gems & Crystals: Golden Topaz, Green-Yellow Tourmaline, Tiger's Eye, Heliodor, Rutilated Quartz, Amber, place stones on the affected area for 15 minutes 3 times a day for 21 days.
IER: after using the tuning forks and Gemstones, have the client breathe into the affected area, press lightly on the affected on the out breath, repeat 3 times.
Reiki: Apply the Reiki with the hands over the stones for 15 minutes

Snoring
Tuning Forks: Use the 3rd, 4th, 5th and 6th Chakra forks and the Oxygen fork over the face area for 15 minutes before bed, seal with the Creation fork.
Gems & Crystals: Citrine, Golden Topaz, Golden Beryl, Aragonite, Orange, Tiger's Eye, Heliodor, Ruby, Hiddenite, Grossular Garnet, Green Jade, place these stones under the pillow for 30 days.
IER: after using the tuning forks and Gemstones, have the client breathe into the chest & abdomen area, press lightly on the abdomen on the out breath, repeat 3 times.
Reiki: Apply the Reiki with the hands over the stones for 15 minutes

Spleen Problems
Tuning Forks: Balance the Chakras, and then use the Spleen fork, Blood fork for 15 minutes each fork, also do the Lymphatic process.
Gems & Crystals: Rose Quartz, Pink Tourmaline, Rubellite, Rhodochrosite, Emerald, Green Tourmaline, lay stones on the area for 15 minutes 3 times a day for 10 days.
IER: after using the tuning forks and Gemstones, have the client breathe into the spleen area, press lightly on the abdomen on the out breath, repeat 3 times.
Reiki: Apply the Reiki with the hands over the stones for 15 minutes

Stomach Problems
Tuning Forks: Balance the Chakras and then use Stomach fork, Colon fork, Bladder fork, Liver fork and use each fork for 5 minutes each, then seal in with the Creation fork.
Gems & Crystals: Heliodor, Rutilated Quartz, Amber, Sunstone, Malachite, Peridot and Emerald, Aragonite, Orange Calcite, Selenite, Zircon lay stones on the stomach area for 15 minutes 3 times a day for 12 days.
IER: after using the tuning forks and Gemstones, have the client breathe into the abdomen area, press lightly on the abdomen on the out breath, repeat 3 times.
Reiki: Apply the Reiki with the hands over the stones for 15 minutes

Stroke
Tuning Forks: Balance the Chakras, and then sue the Brain fork, Circulation fork, and Oxygen fork, use each fork for 5 minutes and then seal in with the Creation fork.
Gems & Crystals: Nephrite, Kunzite, Prehnite, Chrysoprase, Rhodonite, Moldavite, Prasiolite, Watermelon Tourmaline, place the stones on the chest area for 20 minutes 4 times a day for 60 days.

IER: after using the tuning forks and Gemstones, have the client breathe into the chest area, press lightly on the chest on the out breath, repeat 3 times.
Reiki: Apply the Reiki with the hands over the stones for 15 minutes

Swelling (Swollen Glands)
Tuning Forks: Balance the Chakras and the Organs and then sue the Manganese fork for 15 minutes, and then seal in with the Creation fork.
Gems & Crystals: Bloodstone, Aurauralite place stones on the affected area for 12 minutes 3 times a day.
IER: after using the tuning forks and Gemstones, have the client breathe into the affected area, press lightly on the abdomen on the out breath, repeat 3 times.
Reiki: Apply the Reiki with the hands over the stones for 15 minutes

Syphilis
Tuning Forks: Use the 1st, 2nd, 3rd, and 4th Chakra forks and the Bone fork, Brain fork for 5 minutes each fork, then seal in with the Creation fork.
Gems & Crystals: Black Tourmaline, Smoky Quartz, Onyx, Agate, Black Obsidian, Hematite, Fire Agate, Ametrine, Blood Stone, Nephrite, place stones on the 2nd chakra area for 30 minutes, 3 times a day for 34 days.
IER: after using the tuning forks and Gemstones, have the client breathe into the 2nd chakra area, press lightly on the abdomen on the out breath, repeat 3 times.
Reiki: Apply the Reiki with the hands over the stones for 15 minutes

T

Teeth Problems
Tuning Forks: Balance the Chakras and the Organs and then use the Oxygen fork, for 5 minutes waving it over the mouth area, then seal with the Creation fork.
Gems & Crystals: Apophyllite, Aquamarine, Blue Lace Agate, Blue Topaz, Blue Tourmaline, Celestite, Indicolite, Blue Turquoise, place stones along the face of the mouth from the ears to the front of the mouth for 15 minutes 3 times a day for 23 days.
IER: after using the tuning forks and Gemstones, have the client breathe into the mouth area, press lightly on the abdomen on the out breath, repeat 3 times.
Reiki: Apply the Reiki with the hands over the stones for 15 minutes

Thymus
Tuning Forks: Balance the Chakras and then use the Lymphatic process
Gems & Crystals: Yellow Tourmaline, Tiger's Eye, Heliodor, Rutilated Quartz, Amber, Sunstone, Malachite, Peridot and Emerald, lay the stones on the area for 15 minutes 5 times a day for 21 days.
IER: after using the tuning forks and Gemstones, have the client breathe into the thymus area, press lightly on the abdomen on the out breath, repeat 2 times.
Reiki: Apply the Reiki with the hands over the stones for 15 minutes

Thyroid
Tuning Forks: Use the 3rd, and 5th chakra forks, then balance the organs and seal in the session with the Creation fork.
Gems & Crystals: Citrine, Golden Topaz, Golden Beryl, Aragonite, Orange Calcite, Selenite, Zircon, lay stones on the area for 15 minutes 4 times a day.
IER: after using the tuning forks and Gemstones, have the client breathe into the thyroid area, press lightly on the abdomen on the out breath, repeat 3 times.
Reiki: Apply the Reiki with the hands over the stones for 15 minutes

Tuberculosis
Tuning Forks: Balance the Chakras and then use the Lung fork, Nerve fork, and do the Lymphatic process.
Gems & Crystals: Aurauralite, Kunzite, Green Aventurine, Ruby, Hiddenite, Grossular Garnet, Green Jade, place the stones on the chest area for 15 minutes 5 times a day for 21 days.
IER: after using the tuning forks and Gemstones, have the client breathe into the chest area, press lightly on the abdomen on the out breath, repeat 3 times.
Reiki: Apply the Reiki with the hands over the stones for 15 minutes

Tumors
Tuning Forks: Use 3rd and 4th Chakra forks and the Creation fork for 15 minutes each fork wave over the tumor area twice a day.
Gems & Crystals: Citrine, Golden Topaz, Green-Yellow Tourmaline, Tiger's Eye, Heliodor, Rutilated Quartz, Amber, Sunstone, Malachite, Peridot, Emerald, Kunzite, Green Aventurine, Ruby, Hiddenite, Grossular Garnet, Green Jade, lay the stones on area for 30 minutes 2 times a day for 40 days.
IER: after using the tuning forks and Gemstones, have the client breathe into the affected area, press lightly on the abdomen on the out breath, repeat 3 times.
Reiki: Apply the Reiki with the hands over the stones for 15 minutes

U

Ulcers
Tuning Forks: Use 3rd, 4th and 6th Chakra forks along with the Circulation fork, Blood fork and Oxygen fork, then seal with the Creation fork.
Gems & Crystals:
Tiger's Eye, Heliodor, Garnet, Green Jade, Amethyst, Celestite, Tanzanite, Blue Tourmaline, Sapphire, Lavender Quartz, Purple Fluorite, place these stones over the lower abdoman area for 12 minutes 3 times a day for 16 days.
IER: after using the tuning forks and Gemstones, have the client breathe into the lower abdomen area, press lightly on the lower abdomen on the out breath, repeat 3 times.
Reiki: Apply the Reiki with the hands over the stones for 15 minutes

V

Varicose Veins
Tuning Forks: Use the 3rd and 4th chakra forks along with the Oxygen fork, Circulation fork, Blood fork, Muscle fork, use each fork for 5 minutes waving over the affected area, then seal in with the Creation fork.
Gems & Crystals: Citrine, Golden Topaz, Green-Yellow Tourmaline, Aurauralite, Bloodstone, place these stones on the affected area for 20 minutes a day for 30 days.
IER: after using the tuning forks and Gemstones, have the client breathe into the affected area, press lightly on the abdomen on the out breath, repeat 3 times.
Reiki: Apply the Reiki with the hands over the stones for 15 minutes

Venereal Disease
Tuning Forks: Balance the Chakras, and then use the Endocrine and Lymphatic process.
Gems & Crystals: Aurauralite, Bloodstone, Black Tourmaline, Smoky Quartz, Onyx, Agate, Black Obsidian, Hematite, Fire Agate, Ametrine, place the stones on the pubic area for 30 minutes 3 times a day for 30 days.

IER: after using the tuning forks and Gemstones, have the client breathe into the pubic area, press lightly on the abdomen on the out breath, repeat 3 times.
Reiki: Apply the Reiki with the hands over the stones for 15 minutes

W

Wilson's Disease
Tuning Forks: Balance the Chakras and Organs and use the Copper fork, for 10 minutes each day, and then sealing in with the Creation fork.
Gems & Crystals: Place copper over the abdomen for 30 days, 20 minutes each day.
IER: after using the tuning forks and Gemstones, have the client breathe into the abdomen area, press lightly on the abdomen on the out breath, repeat 3 times.
Reiki: Apply the Reiki with the hands over the stones for 15 minutes

Wound Healing
Tuning Forks: Balance the Chakras and the Organs, and then use the Zinc fork for 15 minutes over the wound area waving it in a circular motion, and then seal with the Creation fork.
Gems & Crystals: It is not recommend to use Crystals or Gemstones on wounds at least for 24 hours after the injury, then use Bloodstone, 2 times a day for 7 days.
IER: It is not recommend to use IER on wounds.
Reiki: Apply the Reiki with the hands over the stones for 15 minutes

X

Y

Yeast Infections
Tuning Forks: Use the 1st,2nd,3rd, 4th, and 6th Chakra forks for 5 minutes each over the entire body, then seal in with the Creation fork.
Gems & Crystals: Black Tourmaline, Smoky Quartz, Onyx, Agate, Black Obsidian, Hematite, Fire Agate, Ametrine, Citrine, Golden Topaz, Golden Beryl, Aragonite, Orange Calcite, Selenite, Zircon, use these stone on the lower abdomen area for 15 minutes 3 times a day for 30 days.
IER: after using the tuning forks and Gemstones, have the client breathe into the lower abdomen area, press lightly on the lower abdomen on the out breath, repeat 3 times.
Reiki: Apply the Reiki with the hands over the stones for 15 minutes

Z

AFTERTHOUGHTS

It has been a true joy and very satisfying to compile this collection of levels for Crystal and Gemstone healing. This books has evolved over the years as I have learned more about holistic healing modalities and how best to help people with them. My hope is that any reader of this book walks away with true insight on Crystals and Gemstones in healing as well as how to combine that with other modalities to improve people's wellness. Thank you for reading and if you want to learn more, I have included a section of recommended reading on the next page!

Charles

ADDENDUM & RECOMMENDED READING

There are a variety of resources, which are very helpful when you are working with Crystals and Stones.

Theses books are absolutely invaluable as reference guides in your healing journey with Crystal and Stones.

National Audubon Society field guide to North American Rocks and Minerals. By Alfred A. Knopf, Inc.

Love is in the Earth Mineralogical Pictorial. By Melody

Love is the Earth A Kaleidoscope of Crystals. By Melody

The illustrated Guide to Crystals. By Judy Hall

The Crystal Bible. By Judy Hall

Crystal Medicine. By Marguerite Elsbeth

Healing with Crystals & Gemstones. By Daya Sarai Chocron

The Complete Crystal Guidebook. By Uma Silbey

Crystal Healing Secrets. By Brett Bravo

Crystal Balance. By Monika Grundmann

Gemstone Reflexology. By Nora Kircher

The Crystal Healer. By Philip Permntt

Divine Dining. By Catherine Russo Epstein

Crystals By Jennie Harding

About the Author

After sustaining a major injury whilst serving in the united states military, Charles Lightwalker sought out alternative methods of healing and went down a long learning journey of alternative medicinal techniques and spiritual counseling. Charles quickly realised that he wanted to pursue a career along this path and that he could use his intuitive gifts to help others as he had been helped. Charles has experience with doing reiki, spiritual counseling, and medical intuition. He also has taught classes as well as written numerous books on these subjects over the years, as well as on other topics such as using tuning forks, holistic healing, and other metaphysical subjects. In his downtime, Charles enjoys doing yoga, meditating, writing, and strolling along the beaches of Scotland, which is where he currently resides with his family.

www.ingramcontent.com/pod-product-compliance
Lightning Source LLC
Chambersburg PA
CBHW042019090526
44590CB00029B/4337